Super Simple
OUTDOOR
COOKBOOK

Quick and Easy Food for Outdoor Fun

....
LINDA LY
....

NEW SHOE PRESS

Quarto.com

© 2023 Quarto Publishing Group USA Inc.
Text © 2017, 2019 Lynda Ly
Photography © 2017, 2019 Will Taylor

First Published in 2023 by New Shoe Press, an imprint of The Quarto Group,
100 Cummings Center, Suite 265-D, Beverly, MA 01915, USA.
T (978) 282-9590 F (978) 283-2742

New Shoe Press titles are also available at discount for retail, wholesale, promotional, and bulk purchase. For details, contact the Special Sales Manager by email at specialsales@quarto.com or by mail at The Quarto Group, Attn: Special Sales Manager, 100 Cummings Center, Suite 265-D, Beverly, MA 01915, USA.

ISBN: 978-0-7603-8374-2
eISBN: 978-0-7603-8375-9

The content in this book appeared in the previously published titles *The New Camp Cookbook* (Voyageur Press, 2017) and *The Backyard Fire Cookbook* (The Harvard Common Press, 2019) and *The Ultimate Outdoor Cookbook* (The Harvard Common Press, 2021).

Library of Congress Cataloging-in-Publication Data available

Photography: Will Taylor
Illustration: Shutterstock.com

Contents

Introduction

When I close my eyes and think of my happy place, I picture this: a canopy of conifers with a breeze whipping through, a bubbling creek, or perhaps a glassy lake, with a sublime string of peaks in the distance. Tents and coolers. Logs and embers. A hot, hearty meal shared around the fire with family and friends as the last light fades.

It's no secret I love a good campfire, but, above all, I love a great meal cooked over one. I love the leap and snap of a lively fire as it collapses into red-hot coals. I love the alchemy of sun and smoke that makes those long summer days seem even slower. I love the fact that every time you grill and gather around a fire, it's a community event. You pull up your chairs, clink some cold libations, and sink into conversations that get longer and deeper as the night goes on.

With a live fire, you're not just turning a knob to medium-high and waiting patiently for your food to brown. You're not merely cooking—you're conducting: feeding the flames, moving the coals, or fine-tuning the vents, guiding the grill to a perfect harmony of char and smoke.

In this book, you're not going to find low and slow barbecue or overnight brines, or whole animals tied to iron crosses or spinning on a spit. These are recipes you can make on those low-key nights when you just want to sit in the backyard with a drink in hand, enjoying the colors of a softening sky and the smells of good food sizzling on the grill.

Away from home and under the open sky, cooking is stripped down to the bare essentials, so food becomes its own adventure—but don't mistake adventure to mean nerve-wracking or hard. Cooking in camp can be as easy or extravagant as you want it to be, but the experience in itself triggers all the senses, making you feel alive and free. There's a definite pleasure in escaping from our reliance on our kitchens, with their sleek appliances and specialized gadgets, and delving deep into our instincts—taming the flames and guiding the elements of nature to a delicious end.

Every time you make a meal or even a single recipe, it may very well turn out a little different than the last time. It could be the brand of charcoal or type of firewood you use, the salty air near the sea, the elevation of your campsite, or the fresh green scent of conifers blowing through the forest. And that's what keeps it so exciting.

Whether you're out for the day or gone on a weeklong road trip, whether you're traveling in a tricked-out trailer with a fully stocked kitchen or sleeping in a whisper-light tent with fire and foil as your primary mode of dinner, this book aims to equip you with the right tools and a repertoire of adaptable recipes for planning, packing, cooking, and eating well in the great outdoors.

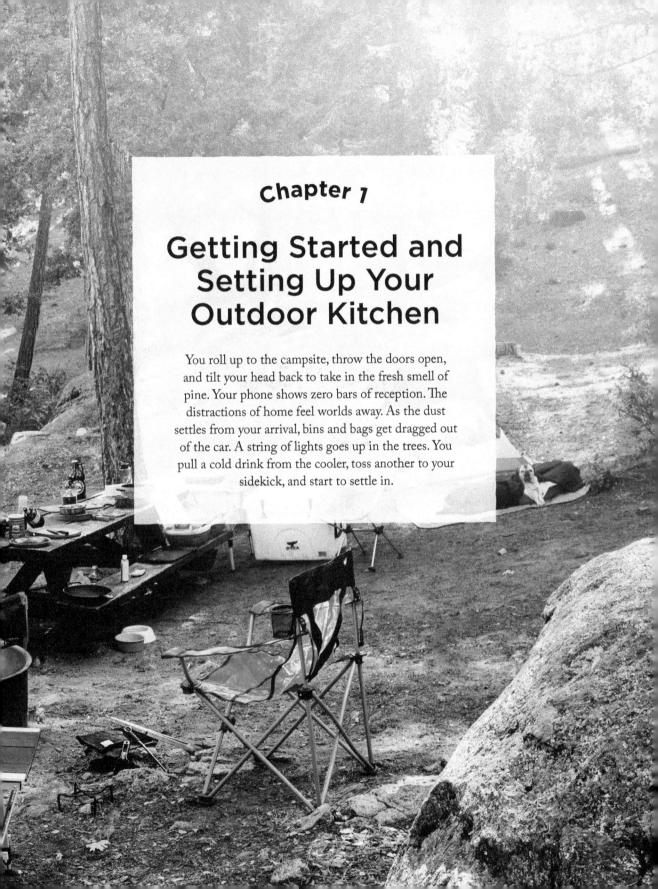

Chapter 1

Getting Started and Setting Up Your Outdoor Kitchen

You roll up to the campsite, throw the doors open, and tilt your head back to take in the fresh smell of pine. Your phone shows zero bars of reception. The distractions of home feel worlds away. As the dust settles from your arrival, bins and bags get dragged out of the car. A string of lights goes up in the trees. You pull a cold drink from the cooler, toss another to your sidekick, and start to settle in.

Build the Ultimate Cooking Fire

While I love my charcoal grill for the speed and convenience it offers, I leap at the chance to cook over a wood fire if the timing is right and an eager crowd is pulling up their chairs (because what fun is fire without family and friends to share it with?).

Building a fire is also much easier than survival shows make it seem. As long as you have something to start the fire with and a stack of clean seasoned wood, you can get a nice fire going in less time than it takes to finish a tasty cold beverage.

How to Make an Old-School Campfire

To allow plenty of time for the fire to burn down into a bed of hot, glowing coals, start your fire at least 45 minutes to 1 hour before you plan to grill.

Step 1: Loosely pile a couple large handfuls of tinder in the center of your fire pit. Make a small teepee around the tinder with the kindling, leaning the sticks against each other for support.

Step 2: Make a second teepee around the first teepee with your smaller logs. Remember to leave a little gap at the bottom so you can reach in easily with a lighter.

Step 3: Light the tinder. As the wood starts burning, continue to add more logs, leaving space for airflow and gradually increasing the size of the logs until the fire is firmly established.

Step 4: Once the logs burn down into ashy red embers, gently break them apart with a grill rake. Rake a large mound of coals toward the front of the fire pit to cook with and keep a small fire going in the back to replenish the coals as needed.

The Three Stages of Building a Wood-Burning Fire

1. Tinder: In a backyard setting, this is usually crumpled paper or a fire starter. You can even get creative with other super combustible materials, such as dryer lint or paper egg cartons.

2. Kindling: Once the tinder catches fire, it needs kindling to keep the flames going. A pile of small sticks, twigs, and branches burns just long enough to light the next stage of your fire.

3. Logs: The kindling lights the logs on top as it starts to burn down. With proper airflow around the logs and a steady supply of firewood, a fire can be maintained from the first course all the way through dessert and beyond.

GRILL HACK

To turn your charcoal grill into a wood-burning grill, fill a chimney with chunks of smoking wood and light them, just as you would light charcoal. As the wood burns down into embers, add more wood to top up the chimney.

How to Light a Chimney

With a chimney starter, you can light a full load of charcoal at once with very little effort.

Step 1: Remove the top (cooking) grate from your charcoal grill and open all the dampers. (You only need the bottom charcoal grate at this point.) Fill the chimney to the top with charcoal.

Step 2: From here, you have two options to get those coals lit:

• **The traditional way:** Stuff a couple sheets of loosely crumpled newspaper in the bottom compartment of the chimney, then set it on the charcoal grate. Tilt the chimney slightly to encourage airflow and light the paper with a lighter. Stand the chimney upright and wait for the coals to catch.

• **With a fire starter:** Place it on the charcoal grate and light it. Set the chimney directly on top of the fire starter and let the flames do their thing.

Step 3: About 15 to 20 minutes after you light the chimney, flames will dance out the top and the charcoal will start to turn gray with ash. At this stage, the coals should be sufficiently lit to pour into the grill.

HOT TIP

When handling lump charcoal, slip a plastic bag over your hand to keep your fingers clean.

GRILL HACK

No chimney starter? No problem. Open the bottom vent on your grill all the way and place eight to ten sheets of crumpled newspaper (or two or three fire starters) below the bottom grate. Pile the charcoal evenly across the bottom grate and light the paper or fire starters. Once the charcoal is coated in ash, set the top grate in place.

Creating Cooking Zones

Direct heat is hot and fast. You place the food on the grate directly over the coals for a blast of heat that gives it those beautiful grill marks, a burnished crust, and crispy skin. Direct heat is ideal for searing meats and browning vegetables, and for grilling quick-cooking foods such as seafood, bread, and cheese.

Indirect heat is moderate and slow. The food is placed on the grate over a heat-free zone and cooked by the heat of the coals banked on the side. This allows slower-cooking foods (such as whole chickens and hefty cuts of pork and beef) more time to cook through on the inside without burning on the outside.

Single-Level Fire

Spread an even layer of coals, one or two coals deep, across the bottom of a fire pit or grill. This creates a medium-hot fire that's the sweet spot for direct grilling most foods. Adjust the thickness of the layer to reduce or increase the heat as needed.

Two-Zone Fire

Bank all the coals to one side of the fire pit or grill, leaving the other side empty for a completely cool zone. This versatile arrangement allows for direct and indirect grilling, as well as a coal-free zone if your food is charring too quickly or causing flare-ups. Aim to leave at least one-third of the grill empty as a safety zone or warming rack.

Three-Zone Fire

Bank the coals to each side of the grill and leave the middle empty. This creates an indirect cooking zone in the center of the grill with heat coming from both sides, allowing your food to cook evenly without the need to rotate halfway through.

Single-level fire

Two-zone fire

Three-zone fire

HOT TIP

While small flames are fine, you don't want your food engulfed in fire, no matter how awesome it looks. Wait until the wood burns down into glowing red coals, which gives you more control over the heat.

How Hot Are the Coals?

For direct grilling, the easiest way to gauge the temperature of your grilling surface is with your hand—no matter how high the grate sits above the coals. Though this may sound even less precise than relying on a thermometer, much of grilling is based on your senses, and holding your hand above the grate will give you a better sense of heat.

The Hand Check

Hover your hand about 3 inches (7.5 cm) above the cooking grate. Count the number of seconds you can hold your hand there comfortably before you have to pull back.

Refueling Your Cooking Fire

If your recipe calls for a cooking time of more than 30 minutes, it's a good idea to have more coals ready so you can maintain steady heat.

TIME	HEAT LEVEL	GRILL TEMPERATURE
1 to 2 seconds	Hot	450°F to 550°F (230°C to 290°C)
2 to 4 seconds	Medium-hot	400°F to 425°F (200°C to 220°C)
4 to 5 seconds	Medium	350°F to 375°F (180°C to 190°C)
More than 5 seconds	Medium-low to low	Ideal for warming (these lower temperatures are also where smoking, or true barbecue, comes in)

For a wood fire, simply keep a small fire going in the back of the fire pit and periodically feed it with more logs to produce more coals. Rake the coals over to your cooking area as needed.

For a charcoal fire, scatter a few chunks of unlit hardwood lump charcoal on top of the embers. Leave the grill lid open for a few minutes until the fresh charcoal catches fire.

How to Dispose of Wood Ash

With a **charcoal grill,** good grilling habits include emptying the ash catcher before (or after) each use. I like to empty mine before I start grilling, as the ashes from the previous session will have cooled for at least 24 hours. Carefully remove the ash catcher and dump the contents into an ash bucket with a tight-fitting lid. Let the ashes cool completely for several days, after which they can be used in the garden, disposed of in a green waste bin, or placed in the trash.

With a **fire pit,** let the ashes cool for at least 24 hours so they're safer to handle. Collect the ashes into an ash bucket to cool for several days, then use them in the garden or place them in a green waste bin or trash can.

Start Grilling

Now that you know how to build a fire in a fire pit (see page 8), how to light a chimney (see page 9), how to create cooking zones (see page 10), and how to gauge the temperature of your grilling surface (see page 11), it's time to put it all together!

Step 1: Fire it up: If you're going to cook over a wood fire, give it at least 45 minutes to 1 hour to burn down into glowing embers. If you're going to cook over charcoal, light the chimney at least 20 minutes before you want to start grilling.

Step 2: Arrange the coals: Once all the coals are lightly covered in gray ash, use a grill rake to arrange them into a single-level, two-zone, or three-zone fire. Set the cooking grate in place, if using, and let it preheat for about 10 minutes. If you're working with a charcoal grill, adjust the vents as needed to reach your desired temperature. (Learn more about venting on page 89.)

Step 3: Clean and oil the grate: There are several ways to clean a grate, with my favorite being a Grate Chef Grill Wipe for its effectiveness and convenience. If you've neglected to clean the grate after your last grilling session, start with a good scrub using a grill brush when the grate is hot (as the heat helps release any food remnants). Aside from oiling the grate, the wipe picks up any greasy residue left behind by the brush, as well as possible stray brush bristles.

As an alternative to a grill wipe, you can do it the old-fashioned way: wad up a paper towel (or some aluminum foil), hold it with tongs, mist the towel with high-heat cooking spray, and wipe down the hot grate.

Another fun method for cleaning and oiling a grate is to use an onion. Cut a small onion in half, spear it with a barbecue fork, and mist the cut side with high-heat cooking spray. Rub the onion firmly over the hot grate. The juices and oil work to loosen any burnt-on bits, wipe away grime, and lubricate the grate.

If you're grilling corn, shuck the ears and save the green husks. Wad up the husks, grip the wad with tongs, and mist with high-heat cooking spray. Watch your friends marvel at your ingenuity as you clean and oil the grill with it!

Step 4: Finally, food! When it's time to place the food on the grate, here are a few of my favorite tips for grilling more efficiently:

- **Arrange the food in a logical fashion.** Place pieces from left to right (or back to front) so you know what went on first and what might need to be turned first or come off the grill first.

- **Don't overcrowd the grate.** Leave at least 1 to 2 inches (2.5 to 5 cm) of space between pieces of food so the sides cook evenly and you have room to work.

- **Grill on the diagonal.** If you want professional-looking grill marks on your steaks, chops, or other flat, wide foods, place them diagonal to the bars on the grate. After a couple of minutes, rotate the food a quarter turn to make a handsome crosshatch of grill marks.

- **Make the most of your fire by using it to the very end.** Throw on a few vegetables to round out your meal or grill other food to save for lunch the next day. If your fire has gotten very low, remove the grate and put some onions, garlic, or elephant garlic directly on the embers to roast while you eat.

Step 5: Clean and oil the grate again: The last thing you probably want to do after you cook is clean, but a quick swipe of a grill brush (while the grate is still hot) can save you a lot of elbow grease in the end. Just run the brush over the grate a few times to dislodge any debris and continue with your meal. You can return to the grill at the end of the day (or even the next morning) to polish it off with a grill wipe.

WARNING

Avoid spraying oil directly onto a grate as it's heating up.

When Is It Done?

With heat being variable across different fire pits and grills, not to mention the type of wood or charcoal used, and even how the weather is that day, you can't always trust the timing in any particular recipe.

See. A lot of what you need to know is in plain sight: the blackened kernels on an ear of corn, the deep brown crust on a scallop, the glistening char on chicken skin, or the tone of red inside that shows you how well the steak is done.

Hear. That oh-so-satisfying hiss of a burger landing on the grill, or the steady hum of a stew bubbling in a Dutch oven, are good indicators that tell you how high or low the heat is.

Smell. Properly grilled food has an intoxicating aroma deeply rooted in our ancestral history: warm, earthy, smoky, caramelized, sometimes evoking hints of sage or grass.

Touch. How something feels is important, too: the tenderness of charred vegetables, the crispness of pizza crust, or the gentle give of bread pudding and pancakes.

Taste. And, of course, that first bite will always let you know whether your food needs more or (needed!) less time on the grill.

Grilling Temperatures for Meats

The United States Department of Agriculture (USDA) and other national food safety agencies have official recommendations for "safe" cooking temperatures, but my preferences are sometimes lower or higher than their guidelines. If you choose to go lower for some meats (steak is a good example), you need to balance your desire for more favorable textures with safety. On the other hand, while dark meat chicken is safe to eat at 165°F (74°C), I find it is at its juiciest and most tender at higher temperatures, when the heat has had time to break down tough connective tissue.

BEEF	TEMPERATURE
Rare	115°F to 120°F; 120°F to 125°F after resting (46°C to 49°C; 49°C to 52°C after resting)
Medium-rare	120°F to 125°F; 125°F to 130°F after resting (49°C to 52°C; 52°C to 54°C after resting)
Medium	130°F to 135°F; 135°F to 140°F after resting (54°C to 57°C; 57°C to 60°C after resting)
Medium-well	140°F to 145°F; 145°F to 150°F after resting (60°C to 63°C; 63°C to 65.5°C after resting)
Well-done	150°F to 155°F; 155°F to 160°F after resting (65.5°C to 68°C; 68°C to 71°C after resting)

PORK	TEMPERATURE
Medium	140°F to 145°F; 150°F after resting (60°C to 63°C; 65.5°C after resting)
Well-done	150°F to 155°F; 160°F after resting (65.5°C to 68°C; 71°C after resting)

CHICKEN	TEMPERATURE
White meat	165°F (74°C)
Dark meat	180°F to 185°F (82°C to 85°C)

Carryover Cooking

When you take the meat off the grill, heat on the meat's surface continues to travel inward, causing the internal temperature of the meat to rise. It's also an important reason you should take meats off the grill *before* they reach your target temperature for doneness, as they continue to rise 5 to 10 degrees while resting.

Meats with more thermal mass, such as roasts and thick cuts of steak, absorb more heat during grilling and have a greater amount of carryover. Thin cuts, like skirt steaks, don't have time to build up a large heat reservoir so there is very little carryover. While carryover cooking can also occur in poultry, it's best to cook chicken to proper doneness for safety reasons.

The Importance of Resting

When meat is left to sit after being taken off the grill, the muscle fibers relax and allow the internal juices to redistribute throughout the roast or cut.

Steaks benefit from 5 to 10 minutes of rest while large roasts need at least 15 minutes. Combined with carryover cooking, resting helps ensure your food is cooked perfectly to your taste.

I usually let steaks rest as I plate them for my guests.

Fire Safety

To make sure the fire stays *inside* the grill, keep these safety points in mind.

- Don't grill under eaves or overhangs, patio covers, tree branches, or other combustible objects.
- Pay attention when grilling on a wooden deck or in an area with a lot of dry grass and bushes. If needed, hose down those areas with water before you start grilling.
- Pay extra attention in windy weather, as sparks can fly off the grill.
- If you have a fire pit, it's a good idea to keep a bucket of sand nearby for smothering grease fires.
- With open fire pits, have a reliable water source handy in case you need to douse floating embers.
- Keep a large box of salt or baking soda on hand for smothering small grease fires in a grill. A little refrigerator-size carton is not going to cut it.

- And, most importantly, get a Class K, B, or ABC fire extinguisher and know how to use it. Service it annually and check the pressure gauge periodically to ensure it's in working order.

Preventing Flare-Ups

You can control flare-ups by trimming excess fat from meats, patting excess oil from marinated meats with a paper towel, or using a two-zone fire for cooking. If a flare-up occurs, simply move the meat to the cool (empty) side of the grill until the fire dies down, then move it back over direct heat to finish cooking. Closing the grill lid will also control minor flare-ups by snuffing out the flames.

What to Do If Your Grill Catches Fire

Sometimes, the grease that accumulates at the bottom of your grill (in a drip pan, for instance) or on a plancha can catch fire. Act fast! Close the grill lid to contain the flames. Slide the dampers shut to starve the fire of oxygen and wait for it to burn out.

For small grease fires, you can also try smothering them with salt or baking soda. It takes a lot of salt or baking soda to do this, so keep a full box stashed in your outdoor kitchen. (Note that other baking products, like baking powder or flour, will not help and will only make the fire worse.)

> **WARNING**
>
> **Never use water to put out a grease fire.** Pouring water on the flames can cause the oil to splash and spread the fire farther.

Cooking on a Camp Stove

Whether it's boiling water for your morning coffee or stir-frying vegetables for a family dinner, a good camp stove lets you cook anything in camp that you typically cook at home.

While camp stoves offer a narrow window of adjustability from low to high heat, wind and cold weather outside can greatly affect the output of the flame. A more accurate way to measure heat on a cooking surface—in the absence of a cooking thermometer—is with your hand. (See *The Hand Check* on page 11.)

Food and Forest Safety

As with any outdoor situation, you can never be too prepared or cautious, especially if you're camping with a large group where small details may be overlooked.

Handling and Preparing Food Safely

Since sanitation is limited in camp, it's important to maintain a scrupulously clean kitchen. The safety precautions you take when cooking at home don't change when you're cooking in camp—they become even more important.

When it comes to food safety, these five key points should always be in the front of your mind:

- Keep your cooler at 40°F (4°C) or below at all times. (Bring a fridge thermometer for peace of mind.)

- Never leave food out for a prolonged period of time. If food is sitting in the "danger zone" between 40°F and 140°F (4°C and 60°C), it needs to be used within 2 hours (and discarded after that). Keep it in the cooler, warm it on the stove, or use other methods to keep cold foods cold and hot foods hot within that time frame.

- Cook all meats to proper internal temperatures.

- Avoid cross-contamination between raw meats and other foods.

- Always wash your hands before and after handling food.

- Use a separate meat cooler if possible, or place raw meats in the bottom of a cooler to prevent their juices from dripping onto other food.

- Securely bag or double-bag all raw meats, or store them in watertight containers.

- Keep raw meats away from other food and use separate cutting boards and utensils when working with them.

- Discard used marinades immediately, or boil them for 10 minutes before using as a baste or glaze for your meats.

> **WARNING**
>
> **Keep It Clean.** If you have to handle a lot of raw meats or seafood in camp, bring a pair of disposable gloves—it'll keep your hands odor-free and mess-free, and allow you to work more efficiently when water sources may be scarce.

Safe Storage Times for Chilled Foods

The following table lists safe storage times for perishables stored in a cooler at 40°F (4°C) or below.

Raw ground meat and ground poultry	1 to 2 days
Raw beef, veal, pork, and lamb	3 to 5 days
Raw chicken and turkey	1 to 2 days
Bacon	2 weeks (unopened package) 1 week (opened package)
Raw sausage (from meat or poultry)	1 to 2 days
Hard sausage (such as pepperoni or jerky)	3 weeks (opened package)
Hot dogs	2 weeks (unopened package) 1 week (opened package)
Egg, chicken, tuna, ham, and macaroni salads	3 to 5 days
Cooked meat, poultry, and fish	3 to 4 days
Soups and stews	3 to 4 days
Raw fish and shellfish	1 to 2 days
Eggs (raw, in shell)	3 to 5 weeks
Eggs (raw, out of shell)	2 to 4 days
Eggs (hard-boiled)	1 week
Liquid pasteurized eggs and egg substitutes	10 days (unopened) 3 days (opened)
Cooked egg dishes	3 to 4 days
Milk	1 week
Butter	2 weeks
Buttermilk, sour cream, and cream cheese	2 weeks

Safe Internal Temperatures for Cooked Meats

A meat thermometer is useful if you're uncertain when your food is fully cooked. Insert it into the thickest part of the flesh to test for the following USDA-recommended internal temperatures.

Beef, pork, lamb, and veal (roasts, steaks, and chops)	145°F (63°C) and allow to rest for at least 3 minutes
Ground beef, pork, lamb, and veal	160°F (71°C)
Hot dogs	165°F (74°C)
Poultry breast meat and dark meat	165°F (74°C)
Ground poultry	165°F (74°C)

Dishwashing in the Wild

A designated dishwashing station at your campsite makes cleanup a breeze, and uses less water and soap than washing in a sink with running water. Pack the following supplies in your gear bin and you'll always be prepared when it's time to clear the table.

Washtubs. You need at least two large tubs for washing and rinsing. If you camp with a large group and do a lot of dishes, a third tub might come in handy. Plastic tubs that nest are perfect for this purpose, but collapsible tubs or sinks can be more convenient storage-wise.

Dish rack or mesh bag. You can certainly spread your dishes out on the table to dry, but a dish rack keeps everything tidier. Look for racks that fold, collapse, or nest neatly inside your washtubs. If you want to travel light, you can toss all your camping dishes in a mesh bag and hang it from a tree to air-dry.

Kitchen towel. Bring at least one towel for drying dishes, drying your hands, or a multitude of other kitchen tasks.

Scrubby sponge or dish brush. And if you cook with cast iron, a plastic scraper is useful for removing residue from your pan without removing the seasoning.

Biodegradable soap. Stick with a highly concentrated, environmentally friendly soap like Dr. Bronner's or Campsuds. A little goes a long way!

If you asked ten people how to clean dishes in camp, you'll get ten different answers. A lot of it depends on the size of your group and the amenities in your campground, but the following method has always worked for me in the widest variety of situations. Here's how it's done:

1. Scrape. Scrape any food scraps and uneaten food into a trash bag. Give greasy dishes a wipe with a paper towel. The goal is to get as few food remnants as possible in the washtub.

2. Soak. Fill the first washtub with warm water and a few squirts of soap and soak your dishes and utensils. The sooner you do this after a meal, the easier it will be to clean.

3. Wash. Squirt a little more soap on your sponge and get to work.

4. Rinse. Dunk the soapy dishes in the second tub of water to rinse.

5. Dry. Let the clean dishes drip dry.

6. Repeat with pots and pans. Once all the dishware is done, wash and rinse your cookware using the same method. If your pots and pans have a lot of grease or burnt-on bits, pour a little water in them and boil for a few minutes to soften the residue before you start scrubbing.

7. Dispose of the dishwater. Strain the dirty dishwater from the first tub with a fine sieve or mesh screen placed over the second tub. Toss the food particles in the trash. If the campground doesn't have a cleaning facility for gray water disposal, carry the gray water away from camp (at least 200 feet (61 m) from any natural water sources) and fling it far and wide, preferably in a sunny spot so it evaporates quickly. Alternatively, you can dig a hole 6 to 8 inches (15 to 20 cm) deep for dumping all of your gray water so that food smells are contained to one area.

Tips for Camping in Bear Country

- If you're not able to use a bear box or hang your food from a tree, a bear-proof cooler with a padlock can be a wise investment. Stash it at least 100 feet (30.5 m) away (preferably 200 feet (61 m) or more, and downwind) from your campsite when you leave for the day or turn in for the night.

- Avoid storing food, food containers, or other scented items (such as toothpaste and insect repellent) in your car and especially your tent.

- Never leave food unattended. .

- Do not cook next to your tent or leave dirty dishes in camp.

- In isolated areas, leaving a bright light on at night can help deter bears from rummaging through your campsite (but is not a substitute for proper storage and cleanup procedures).

- Food waste should be treated the same as food. If bear-resistant trash cans aren't available in the campground, trash should be stored in a bear box, hung from a tree, or stashed in a secure container and moved at least 100 feet (30.5 m) downwind from camp. Avoid leaving trash bags loose in camp overnight.

- Camping and cooking in grizzly territory requires extra caution. Always check with local rangers about wildlife activity in the areas you visit.

Chapter 2

Starting the Day: Breakfasts

The song of the mountain chickadee cuts through the stillness at dawn. The sun starts to peek over the mountains as the smell of coffee wafts into your tent. You stir in your sleeping bag, feeling the brisk air on your face. A tent unzips, and then another. Footsteps find their way to the sound of food sizzling in a pan. Amid the clinking of spoons against mugs and forks against plates, plans start taking shape.

A new day of adventure beckons.

Blueberry Skillet Scones with Lemon Glaze

Fresh, warm, homemade pastries at camp? Yes, please! Skillet scones are a campside take on Irish soda farls, the traditional quick-cooking breads made the old-fashioned way on a griddle. They're crisp and dry on the outside but soft and dense in the center, and are delicious with a smear of jam or butter served alongside coffee or tea. To make a savory version of these skillet scones, just swap the sugar, lemon zest, and blueberries for shredded Cheddar and chopped scallions.

FOR THE SCONES

2 cups (240 g) Multipurpose Baking Mix (page 22)

¾ cup (180 ml) buttermilk

¼ cup (56 g) butter, melted and cooled, plus more for greasing

3 tablespoons granulated sugar

1 large egg

Zest of 1 large lemon

1 cup (170 g) blueberries

FOR THE GLAZE

½ cup (57 g) powdered sugar

1 tablespoon lemon juice

—

Makes 14 scones

TO MAKE THE SCONES: In a large bowl, stir together the baking mix, buttermilk, butter, granulated sugar, egg, and lemon zest with a large sturdy spoon until a soft, sticky, and shaggy dough forms. Gently fold in the blueberries.

Grease a large skillet with butter and heat it over medium-low heat. Using a large spoon, drop ¼-cupfuls of dough (slightly larger than a golf ball) into the skillet. Arrange them so that the sides of each biscuit are barely touching. You should have 14 scones.

Cover and cook until the scones are golden brown on the bottom, 4 to 5 minutes. Turn each biscuit over with a spoon and continue cooking, covered, for about 5 minutes more until both sides are lightly browned and the scones are fully cooked in the center.

Meanwhile, to make the glaze, whisk together the powdered sugar and lemon juice in a small bowl until well blended. Drizzle the glaze over the warm scones before serving.

USE IT UP

Want to find a recipe for that buttermilk left in the carton? Use it up in Buttermilk Pancakes with Maple, Mascarpone, and Berries (page 28).

Multipurpose Baking Mix

Freshly made baked goods—that don't come out of a box or can—feel like such a luxury in camp, even though their core ingredients couldn't be simpler. But hauling bags of flour, sugar, and leaveners isn't really feasible, nor is all the exact measuring you have to do every time for every recipe. If you bring a large batch of this highly versatile baking mix, however, you can whip up homemade scones (page 20), pancakes (page 28), biscuits, coffee cakes, and other quick breads with ease. It also works in other recipes that call for commercial all-purpose baking mixes. Double or triple the recipe according to your needs.

3 cups (360 g) all-purpose flour

1 tablespoon sugar

1 tablespoon baking powder

1 teaspoon baking soda

1 teaspoon kosher salt

—
Makes 3 cups (360 g)

Combine all of the ingredients in a medium bowl. Transfer to a resealable plastic bag or lidded container and store in a dry, cool place for up to 8 months. Before using, stir the mix around to evenly distribute the ingredients.

NOTE

I use the "scoop and sweep" method for measuring flour: simply scoop a heaping cupful of flour, then level it with a straightedge. If your flour has been sitting in the bottom of a bag or canister for a while, fluff it up with a fork before scooping.

Toasted Instant Oatmeal

Many people have fond memories of starting their morning in camp by firing up the stove and tearing open a little packet of instant oatmeal. But you can actually make your own instant oatmeal quite easily with less cost and more control over quality and flavor. Start with rolled oats (also called old-fashioned oats), put them through a couple of extra steps, and they suddenly get more interesting. Here, a light toast in the oven imparts a nutty flavor to the oats, while whizzing half of them in a food processor gives the cooked oatmeal a creamier texture than rolled oats alone.

4 cups (400 g) rolled oats

¼ cup (50 g) packed brown sugar
(optional, see Note)

1 teaspoon kosher salt

½ teaspoon ground cinnamon
(optional, see Note)

—

Makes 4 cups (450 g)

Preheat the oven to 350°F (180°C or gas mark 4).

Spread the oats on a rimmed baking sheet and bake for 10 to 15 minutes, stirring halfway through, until lightly toasted but not browned. Let cool.

Put half the toasted oats in a food processor and pulse until finely crumbled. Combine all the oats in a large bowl and stir in the sugar, salt, and cinnamon.

Transfer to a resealable plastic bag or lidded container and store in a dry, cool place for up to 1 year. (Alternatively, you can divide the oatmeal into ½-cup [57-g] portions and store them individually to make your own instant oatmeal packets.)

NOTE

If your preference is for savory oatmeal (like Savory Oatmeal with Bacon, Cheddar, and Fried Egg, opposite page) or you like to control the amount of sweetness in each serving, leave out the brown sugar and cinnamon. Conversely, you can also add more sugar if you typically like your oatmeal sweeter.

MIX IT UP

If you're making your own instant oatmeal packets, mix in your favorite flavorings ahead of time and all that's needed when you're ready to cook is a pot of boiling water. Try any combination of dried fruits (dates, apricots, cranberries), freeze-dried fruits (strawberries, blueberries, apples), seeds (chia, flax, hemp), and other add-ins (coconut flakes, candied ginger, powdered milk). I like to keep nuts separate, added only when the oatmeal is done so they retain their crunch.

Savory Oatmeal with Shiitake and Spinach

In this savory spin on oatmeal, the grains give ricelike texture to a hearty, Asian-inspired breakfast bowl that can hold its own at other times of day. Using chicken broth in place of water amps up the umami factor—and you can try this trick for concocting your own savory oatmeal. If you have leftover cooked chicken from the night before, toss that into the pan too.

2 tablespoons olive oil, divided

1 medium shallot, finely chopped

3 cups (700 ml) chicken broth

2 cups (225 g) Toasted Instant Oatmeal (page 23), no added sugar or cinnamon

8 medium shiitake mushrooms, sliced (about 3 ounces)

¼ teaspoon kosher salt

⅛ teaspoon ground black pepper

3 cups (100 g) packed baby spinach

2 tablespoons ponzu sauce, plus more for serving

—
Makes 4 servings

NOTE

Ponzu sauce is a Japanese citrus-based soy sauce found in the ethnic aisle of most well-stocked supermarkets.

Drizzle 1 tablespoon of the oil in a small saucepan over medium-high heat. Add the shallots and cook until they start to turn translucent, about 2 minutes. Add the broth and oatmeal and bring to a boil. Reduce the heat and simmer for about 5 minutes, stirring occasionally, until the oats are cooked to your preferred consistency. Continue to heat just enough to keep warm.

Meanwhile, set a large skillet over medium-high heat and swirl in the remaining 1 tablespoon oil. Add the mushrooms, salt, and pepper. Cook until the mushrooms are soft, 3 to 5 minutes, stirring occasionally. Add the spinach and ponzu, stir to combine, and cook until the spinach is just wilted, about 2 minutes.

Divide the oatmeal, mushrooms, and spinach among 4 bowls and drizzle with a little ponzu before serving.

Savory Pancakes with Scallions, Mushrooms, and Goat Cheese

Who says pancakes have to be sweet? Savory stacks are a surprising offering among the usual sweet treats of breakfast foods, and they seamlessly move into breakfast-for-dinner territory too. It all starts with my baking mix and the rest is up to your imagination. Swap the mushrooms for sun-dried tomatoes or forgo the goat cheese and melt Cheddar into the batter for oozy goodness. If breakfast is a big, fun, and boisterous tradition at your campsite, you can even host a "pancake bar" and offer a variety of add-ins (both sweet and savory) so friends can fill and flip their own.

FOR THE FILLING

4 medium cremini mushrooms, finely chopped

4 scallions, finely chopped

2 tablespoons olive oil

1 tablespoon chopped fresh thyme

½ teaspoon kosher salt

¼ teaspoon ground black pepper

FOR THE PANCAKES

2 cups (240 g) Multipurpose Baking Mix (page 22)

1½ cups (350 ml) milk

2 large eggs

Butter

Goat cheese

—
Makes 4 servings

TO MAKE THE FILLING: In a small bowl, combine the mushrooms, scallions, oil, thyme, salt, and pepper and set aside.

TO MAKE THE PANCAKES: In a large bowl, whisk the baking mix with the milk and eggs until well blended.

Heat a large skillet over medium heat and melt a pat of butter, swirling to coat the surface. Ladle ¼ cup (60 ml) batter at a time into the skillet. Sprinkle 2 heaping tablespoons of the mushroom and scallion mixture over the batter and lightly press it into the pancake as it cooks. Cook until the edges begin to set, about 3 minutes. Flip the pancake and cook the other side until golden brown and completely set, about 2 minutes more.

Serve with a generous pat of butter and a dollop of goat cheese on top.

USE IT UP

Where else can you use thyme if you have to buy a whole bunch of it? Put it in Seared Rib-Eye Steaks with Herbed Board Sauce (page 53), Grilled Pork Medallions with Cherry-Bourbon Sauce (page 84), or Cedar-Planked Tomatoes Stuffed with Mushrooms and Gruyère (page 111).

Buttermilk Pancakes with Maple, Mascarpone, and Berries

Pancakes are a much-loved morning ritual at camp (heck, even at home), but over the years I've seen far too many mixes come out of a box or even a spray can. Pancake mix is one of those things that's just too easy not to make at home, so stir up a batch of my baking mix and treat your tentmates to real, homemade, fresh, and fluffy buttermilk pancakes.

FOR THE PANCAKES

2 cups (240 g) Multipurpose Baking Mix (page 22)

2 cups (475 ml) buttermilk

½ cup (115 g) mascarpone cheese

2 large eggs

Butter

FOR THE TOPPINGS

2 tablespoons powdered sugar

½ cup (115 g) mascarpone cheese

2 cups (150 g) raspberries, blackberries, or blueberries

Maple syrup

—

Makes 4 servings

TO MAKE THE PANCAKES: In a large bowl, whisk together the baking mix, buttermilk, mascarpone, and eggs until well blended.

In a small bowl, stir the powdered sugar into the other ½ cup (115 g) of mascarpone and set aside.

Heat a large skillet over medium heat and melt a pat of butter, swirling to coat the surface. Ladle ¼ cup (60 ml) batter at a time into the skillet. Cook until bubbles break on the surface and the edges of the pancake begin to set, about 3 minutes. Flip and cook the other side until golden brown and completely set, about 2 minutes more. Repeat with the remaining batter. (To keep the pancakes warm, stack and wrap them in foil as they finish cooking.)

Serve with a dollop of the sweetened mascarpone, a handful of berries, and a drizzle of maple syrup on top.

SKEWERS:
TO SOAK OR NOT TO SOAK?

Conventional culinary wisdom says that wooden skewers should be soaked in water before grilling. But does this really help prevent burning? We feel this practice is up for debate—it seems that no matter how long you soak the skewers, the ends are bound to scorch a bit over a hot grill. If you're concerned about the ends of your skewers burning off completely, you can wrap them in foil or, better yet, invest in stainless steel skewers.

Grilled French Toast and Bacon Bites

These breakfast kebabs are a fun take on the traditional French toast and bacon pairing. If your grill is big enough, you can even make French toast for a crowd by doubling the recipe. (Just be sure to bring enough skewers!) Make them a couple of days into your camping trip to give your bread some time to stale. If you're starting with fresh bread but want to make French toast in the morning, cut it the night before and lay the slices out to dry someplace warm and protected, like the dashboard of your car. The bread will lose just enough moisture for the ideal French toast texture.

3 large eggs

1 cup (240 ml) half-and-half or milk

¼ cup (60 ml) spiced rum

1 tablespoon sugar

6 (¾- to 1-inch-thick) slices slightly stale challah, brioche, or country-style bread

8 strips thick-cut bacon

Maple syrup

—

Makes 4 servings

> ### NOTE
> ___
> If you like your bacon smoky and sweet, brush on some maple syrup before grilling, and occasionally brush the slices with more syrup as they cook.

Prepare a grill for two-zone heat (see page 10).

In a wide, shallow dish, whisk together the eggs, half-and-half, rum, and sugar until the custard is very well blended. (You want to avoid any lingering clumps of egg yolk or egg white that will turn into cooked eggs on your French toast.)

Set aside 6 skewers until ready to use. Cut each slice of bread into 1-inch (2.5-cm) chunks. (You should have about 36 pieces.) Arrange the chunks in a single layer in the dish, working in batches if necessary, and soak the bread in the custard for about 10 seconds. Flip and soak the other side for about 10 seconds more until the bread is fully saturated but not falling apart. Thread the bread onto skewers and set aside to drain slightly. Thread the bacon onto the remaining skewers, folding the bacon back and forth accordion-style and piercing through the meaty parts of the bacon rather than the fat.

Grill the bacon over indirect heat, turning occasionally, for 10 to 12 minutes, until the edges are crisp and browned but the centers are still moist.

Grill the bread over direct heat, turning occasionally, for about 5 minutes, or until the surface is dry and golden brown and the centers are cooked through. If the bread is browning too quickly, finish the skewers over indirect heat once they get a good char.

Serve with a drizzle of maple syrup.

Sweet Potato, Apple, and Pancetta Hash

This autumn-inspired breakfast adds a little flair to the basic bacon-and-potato hash by marrying pancetta and sweet potatoes for a dish that's deeper yet more delicate in flavor. You can vary the texture and taste by experimenting with different varieties of sweet potatoes (such as Japanese sweet potatoes, which have hints of chestnut) and apples (ranging from sweet to tart). To make more servings (or if you just really like eggs), simply make more wells in the final step of the recipe.

6 ounces pancetta, cut into small dice

1 small yellow onion, finely chopped

2 medium apples, cored and cut into ½-inch (1-cm) dice (about 1 pound/ 450 g)

2 tablespoons olive oil

2 large sweet potatoes, peeled and cut into ½-inch (1-cm) dice (about 2½ pounds/1 kg)

1 teaspoon red pepper flakes

½ teaspoon kosher salt

¼ teaspoon ground black pepper

2 cups (65 g) packed baby spinach

4 large eggs

—

Makes 4 servings

NOTE

In a well-stocked supermarket, pancetta can be found pre-diced and packaged in the cured meats cooler.

Heat a large skillet over medium-high heat. Add the pancetta and cook until browned and crispy, 5 to 8 minutes, stirring occasionally. Transfer the pancetta to a large plate, reserving the fat in the skillet.

Let the fat reheat for about 1 minute. Add the onion and cook until it starts to turn translucent, 2 to 3 minutes. Stir in the apples and cook until golden brown, 3 to 5 minutes. Transfer the onion and apples to the plate of pancetta.

Reheat the skillet and lightly coat the bottom with the oil. Add the sweet potatoes in a single layer and cook undisturbed until browned on the bottom, about 5 minutes. Sprinkle the red pepper flakes, salt, and pepper on top and continue cooking, stirring occasionally, for 8 to 10 minutes, or until the sweet potatoes are tender.

Return the pancetta, onion, and apples to the skillet and stir to combine. Add the spinach and cook until wilted, 2 to 3 minutes.

Using a spoon, make 4 deep wells in the mixture. Crack an egg into each well, cover the skillet, and cook until the yolks are just set, 8 to 10 minutes. (If you like your yolks less runny, poach for a few additional minutes.)

Bacon-Wrapped Potatoes with Blue Cheese

There's always that one person in camp who loves to wake with the sun, start the coffee, and slowly rouse the others from their tents with the smell of bacon wafting through the air. If that person is you, put these potatoes on the menu. They take a little longer to cook but only a few minutes to assemble, making them the perfect lazy-morning meditation. Serve them as a whole meal in themselves or as a side dish to eggs (and don't stop at breakfast, either—they go great with steaks for dinner).

Olive oil spray

6 strips bacon, cut in half

12 new potatoes (about 1½ pounds/680 g)

Ground black pepper

1 cup (227 g) sour cream

½ cup (56 g) crumbled blue cheese

2 scallions, thinly sliced

Milk (optional)

—
Makes 4 servings

Prepare a mound of wood coals, hardwood lump charcoal, or charcoal briquettes (see page 9). Move about a quart's worth of coals to the cooking pit and arrange them in a ring (see page 71).

Lightly spray a dutch oven with oil. Wrap a strip of bacon tightly around each potato and arrange the wrapped potatoes in a single layer in the oven, bacon seams down. Scatter a few pinches of pepper on top, cover, and place 2 rings of coals on the lid.

Roast over high heat for 40 to 50 minutes, until the bacon is crisp and the potatoes are tender. Replenish the coals as needed to maintain high heat and rotate the oven and lid halfway through for even cooking.

In a medium bowl, combine the sour cream, blue cheese, and scallions. If desired, add a little milk to thin the consistency. Serve as a dip or drizzle for the potatoes.

HOW DID THE DUTCH OVEN GET ITS NAME?

The term **dutch oven** has endured since the early 1700s, though its origin is somewhat of a mystery. It's commonly believed that an Englishman named Abraham Darby traveled to the Netherlands to study the more advanced Dutch process for casting metal cooking vessels. He returned to Britain and eventually developed and patented a superior method that produced thinner and lighter pots than their predecessors. It's possible his "dutch ovens" may have been named for the original Dutch process.

Another theory proposes that the name came from Dutch salesmen who brought their cast metal pots to the American colonies, and yet another suggests the name arose from the pots' popularity among the early "Dutch" (German) settlers of Pennsylvania—**Dutch** being an adaptation of the German word **Deutsch**.

Chapter 3

Feasting ...
Over the Fire

Cooking in a fire pit is as primitive and thrilling as it gets.
You're closer to the fire, you're at the mercy of the weather, and
your family and friends are gathered around for the show. Even
if you end up burning dinner—and you probably will at some
point, as all great grill masters have—it's still a good time for
all. And this is exactly why fire pits are such an appealing entry
to the world of live-fire cooking.

With nothing between you and the flames (well, maybe just a
cooking grate), food becomes an adventure—buried in the ashes,
singed on the coals, or seared over hot metal. The interactive
nature of cooking over fire will make even those ordinary
weeknight meals something to look forward to.

Build Your Own No-Frills Fire Pit

There are many ways to build a fire pit, but this foundational design is easily replicated with inexpensive materials found at your local home improvement store. It can also be started and finished in a single afternoon so you can get grilling the same night!

Before You Begin

- Check local building codes and ordinances as well as neighborhood covenants, conditions, and restrictions to confirm fire pits are allowed on your property.

- Find out what the required setbacks are from structures and property lines.

- Think about how the prevailing winds blow through your yard and place your fire pit in a spot where smoke won't be blowing into your windows.

- Choose a solid, level, and open area away from your house and any low-hanging limbs or other combustible objects.

- Leave enough space around the fire pit—at least 6 feet (180 cm)—from the fire pit to the back legs of your furniture to set up seating comfortably.

Details

This fire pit measures 44 inches (110 cm) in outside diameter, 32 inches (80 cm) in inside diameter, and 15 inches (37.5 cm) in height. If you decide to use different materials, construct your fire pit to a final size between 36 and 44 inches (90 and 110 cm) in diameter, which creates enough room for a good fire but still keeps gatherers close enough to chat.

Materials Needed

- 48 (4 x 11.6 inch, or 10 x 29.5 cm) flagstone retaining wall blocks

- Lava rocks, gravel, or sand

Step 1: Clear and level the ground of grass, weeds, rocks, and other debris down to the bare dirt. Rake it smooth and tamp down on the dirt to compact it as much as possible. Level it again to make sure your fire pit doesn't turn out lopsided.

Step 2: Set the first layer of the fire pit by arranging 12 blocks in a ring. Every other block, leave a small gap about 2 inches (5 cm) wide to allow for proper airflow.

Step 3: Continue laying the blocks in a ring, using 12 blocks per layer and staggering the joints for structural support. Gradually tighten the size of the gaps as you build up the layers until the top (and last) layer of blocks is fully touching with no gaps.

Step 4: Cover the bottom of the fire pit with a 4-inch (10 cm) base of lava rocks, gravel, or sand to help provide drainage. While you can certainly make a fire over dirt, having drainage allows your fire pit to always be ready for use. Otherwise, you may find it full of dirty ash water a day or two after it rains. I also like to cover the ground surrounding the fire pit with the same rock or gravel, which helps keep dust down and prevent the fire from accidentally spreading.

Step 5: Light your first fire, kick back, and relax! (See page 8 for more on starting and managing the fire.)

Smoky Ember-Roasted Eggplant Dip

If you like baba ghanoush, you'll love this campfire take on the classic Mediterranean dip. The embers add a smoky depth of flavor you simply can't replicate in the oven. When nestled in the coals, the eggplants blister and blacken to the point where they almost look carbonized. But once you open them, you'll find flesh that's supple, savory, and almost meaty. They are just as good eaten like this, perhaps with a spicy tomato sauce slathered on top, or puréed into a smoke-kissed dip you can serve with grilled flatbread or baguette.

3 globe eggplants (about 3 pounds, or 1.35 kg, total)

1 red onion, unpeeled

2 garlic cloves, chopped

¼ cup (60 ml) olive oil, plus more for drizzling

¾ teaspoon kosher salt, plus more for seasoning

¼ cup (60 g) tahini

2 tablespoons (30 ml) fresh lemon juice

¼ teaspoon ground cumin

Handful minced fresh parsley, plus more for garnishing

Smoked paprika, for garnishing

—

Makes 3 to 4 cups (750 g to 1 kg)

Prepare a hot single-level fire in a fire pit (see page 10) and spread the coals into a flat, uniform bed at least 2 inches (5 cm) deep.

Prick the eggplants in several places with a fork.

Place the eggplants and red onion directly on the coals. Grill, turning occasionally, until the eggplants have collapsed, their flesh is very soft, and the skins are charred all over, about 20 minutes for the eggplants and 30 minutes for the onion. Transfer the vegetables to a cutting board and let cool.

Halve the eggplants lengthwise. Scoop out the flesh and place it in a mesh strainer. (It's fine to leave some of the burnt bits on, as they add flavor.) Let drain for at least 15 minutes, mashing the flesh with the back of a spoon as needed to release excess liquid.

Meanwhile, trim and peel the onion. Coarsely chop it and transfer to a food processor. Add the garlic, olive oil, and salt. Pulse into a chunky purée. Add the eggplant, tahini, lemon juice, and cumin. Pulse until the ingredients are combined but still have some texture. Taste and add more salt, as desired.

Transfer the baba ghanoush to a medium bowl and stir in the parsley. Drizzle with a little olive oil, sprinkle a pinch of paprika on top, and garnish with parsley before serving.

WHAT ELSE CAN YOU COOK IN THE EMBERS?

Most self-contained vegetables that have a good amount of moisture inside are ideal candidates for the low and slow method of roasting in ashes, particularly if they're buried under a fire. Think garlic, potatoes, sweet potatoes, and winter squash.

Other vegetables with a sacrificial layer that can be stripped away before eating do well when cooked on top of the coals. Try artichokes, beets, cabbage, eggplant, fennel, leeks, onion, sweet and hot peppers, and sweet corn.

Smaller, more delicate vegetables that need only a kiss of smoke and a blast of heat benefit from a quick sear on the coals to intensify their flavor, such as asparagus and shishito and Padrón peppers.

Ember-Roasted Acorn Squash with Charred Poblanos, Cotija, and Crema

With their thick burly skins, acorn squash are perfectly suited for ember grilling. They roast right in their own shells while retaining their moisture and infusing with the lovely aroma of wood smoke. The result is a squash so buttery you can slice it open and eat it with a spoon! Any winter squash will work for this recipe, including kabocha, kuri, butternut, or plain ol' pumpkin. If you like a spicier kick, throw another pepper into the embers to divvy up among the squash bowls.

2 (1-pound, or 454 g) acorn squash

4 poblano peppers

Kosher salt

Ground black pepper

⅓ to ½ cup (41 to 61 g) crumbled Cotija cheese

⅓ to ½ cup (80 to 120 ml) crema Mexicana

Finely chopped fresh cilantro, for garnishing

—
Makes 4 servings

Prepare a hot single-level fire in a fire pit (see page 10) and spread the coals into a flat, uniform bed at least 2 inches (5 cm) deep. Keep a small fire going in the back of the fire pit to replenish the coals, as needed.

Nestle the squash into the coals. Roast for about 45 minutes, turning every 10 to 15 minutes, until the skin is evenly and lightly charred and the flesh is tender.

Arrange the peppers directly on the coals. Cook for about 10 minutes, until the skin is charred all over, turning occasionally. Remove the peppers from the heat and place them in a plastic bag. Let them sweat for 5 to 10 minutes. Transfer the peppers to a cutting board to cool. Peel and discard the skin. Halve the peppers lengthwise and remove the core and seeds. Chop the peppers into bite-size pieces. Cover to keep warm until the squash is done.

When a skewer easily pierces the thickest part of the squash, transfer them to a cutting board. Halve each squash lengthwise and scoop out and discard the seeds. Season to taste with salt and pepper and divide among four bowls.

Top each squash with an equal amount of peppers and cheese. Serve with a drizzle of crema and a sprinkle of cilantro.

Grilled Panzanella

This Tuscan bread salad truly takes advantage of beautiful summer produce. While traditional panzanella is centered on the best tomatoes you can find, I like to mix it up with other nightshades—almost like a ratatouille in panzanella form.

FOR THE SALAD

1 pound (454 g) mixed tomatoes

1 teaspoon kosher salt, plus more for seasoning

2 zucchini, halved lengthwise

2 bell peppers, any color or a mix, trimmed, cored, and halved lengthwise

1 globe eggplant, cut crosswise into 1-inch (2.5 cm) slices

1 red onion, cut crosswise into 1-inch (2.5 cm) slices

Olive oil cooking spray, for preparing the vegetables

Ground black pepper

1 loaf artisan bread, halved horizontally (as if for a large sandwich)

½ cup (18 g) packed fresh basil leaves, chopped

FOR THE DRESSING

½ cup (120 ml) olive oil

2 tablespoons (18 g) capers, drained

2 garlic cloves, minced

2 tablespoons (30 ml) red wine vinegar

1 tablespoon (15 g) Dijon mustard

½ teaspoon kosher salt

¼ teaspoon ground black pepper

—
Makes 4 to 6 servings

TO MAKE THE SALAD: Prepare a medium-hot single-level fire in a fire pit (see page 10) with a grill grate over the coals.

Halve the tomatoes (if using cherry tomatoes) or cut into ½-inch (1 cm) wedges (if using slicing tomatoes). Place the tomatoes in a bowl large enough to hold the salad. Toss the tomatoes with the salt. Set aside.

Mist the zucchini, bell peppers, eggplant, and red onion with cooking spray. Season both sides with salt and pepper.

Arrange the vegetables on the grate. Grill for 4 to 6 minutes per side, until tender and lightly charred. Remove each vegetable as it's finished and transfer to a cutting board.

Mist both sides of the bread halves with cooking spray. Arrange the bread on the grate. Grill until brown and crispy, 30 seconds to 1 minute per side.

Chop the grilled vegetables into bite-size pieces and add them to the bowl of tomatoes.

Cut the bread into 1-inch (2.5 cm) chunks. Add 6 heaping cups (225 g) of bread along with the basil to the bowl and toss to combine. (Reserve any remaining bread for another use.)

TO MAKE THE DRESSING: In a small bowl, whisk the olive oil, capers, garlic, vinegar, mustard, salt, and pepper until well blended. Pour three-fourths of the dressing over the salad and toss to coat. Let the salad sit for at least 15 minutes for the bread to soak up all the flavors from the dressing and vegetables. Taste and add more dressing, if desired.

Cumin-Crusted Chicken Tacos with Smoky Salsa Verde

When it comes to chicken, I'm all about the dark meat. It's more tender, more flavorful, and less likely to taste like cardboard from overcooking. Chicken thighs also cook quickly and take well to higher temperatures, making them ideal for weeknight grilling. Don't be shy with the cumin seasoning—the chicken can take it, and the tangy tomatillo salsa tempers the bold spice. You'll have enough salsa left to serve with tortilla chips!

FOR THE SALSA VERDE

1½ pounds (681 g) tomatillos, husked

1 white onion, halved lengthwise, root left intact, coarsely chopped

2 jalapeño peppers

Olive oil cooking spray, for preparing the vegetables

½ cup (8 g) packed fresh cilantro

Juice of 1 lime

½ teaspoon kosher salt, plus more as needed

FOR THE CHICKEN TACOS

2 tablespoons (12 g) cumin seeds, coarsely crushed

1 teaspoon kosher salt, plus more for seasoning

½ teaspoon ground black pepper, plus more for seasoning

2 pounds (908 g) boneless, skinless chicken thighs, trimmed of excess fat

2 red onions, quartered, roots left intact

Olive oil cooking spray, for preparing the onion

Warmed flour or corn tortillas, for serving

Toppings of choice
(I recommend thinly sliced radishes, sliced avocado, and chopped fresh cilantro)

Makes 4 servings

Prepare a medium-hot two-zone fire in a fire pit (see page 10) with a grill grate over the coals.

TO MAKE THE SALSA VERDE: Mist the tomatillos, onion, and jalapeños with cooking spray. Arrange the vegetables on the grate over direct heat. Grill for about 8 minutes, until tender and charred, turning occasionally. Remove each vegetable as it's finished and transfer to a cutting board.

Trim and coarsely chop the grilled onion. Stem and core the grilled jalapeños.

In a food processor, combine the chopped onion and jalapeños, tomatillos, cilantro, lime juice, and salt. Pulse until the ingredients are combined into a sauce but still have a slightly chunky consistency. Taste and add more salt, if desired. Transfer to a small bowl. Set aside until ready to use. (The salsa can also be made up to 5 days in advance and refrigerated in an airtight container.)

TO MAKE THE CHICKEN TACOS: In a small bowl, stir together the cumin seeds, salt, and pepper. Season the chicken on all sides with the spice mix.

Mist the red onions with cooking spray and season with a few pinches of salt and pepper.

Arrange the chicken and red onions on the grate over direct heat. Grill the chicken for 10 to 12 minutes, turning occasionally, until evenly charred on both sides and an instant-read thermometer inserted into the thickest part

of the thigh reaches 180°F to 185°F (82°C to 85°C). (Move the chicken over indirect heat if it seems to be burning before it reaches temperature.) Grill the onions until tender and charred, about 8 minutes, turning occasionally.

Slice the chicken and trim and slice the onion.

Assemble a taco bar with the chicken, onions, tortillas, salsa verde, and toppings of choice. Invite guests to serve themselves.

Italian Burgers with Basil Mustard and Giardiniera

A medley of Italian ingredients —Makes this a standout burger for your next backyard gathering. This recipe incorporates the cheese into the meat—this time by pressing it between two thin patties, which keeps the whole thing creamy and moist. Though the meat is usually the star of any burger, the topping is what makes this one truly special.

1½ cups (336 g) Homemade Giardiniera (page 50), plus more for serving

3 tablespoons (45 g) Dijon mustard

1½ tablespoons (21 g) mayonnaise

3 tablespoons (7.5 g) thinly sliced fresh basil

1 pound (454 g) ground chuck

12 ounces (340 g) bulk hot Italian sausage

¾ teaspoon kosher salt

¼ teaspoon ground black pepper

4 slices provolone cheese

4 ciabatta rolls, split

—
Makes 4 servings

At least 3 days before you plan to serve the burgers, make the giardiniera (page 50).

Prepare a medium-hot two-zone fire in a fire pit (see page 10) with a grill grate over the coals.

Finely chop the giardiniera. Set aside until needed.

In a small bowl, stir together the mustard, mayonnaise, and basil. Set aside.

In a large bowl, combine the ground chuck, Italian sausage, salt, and pepper. With clean hands, lightly mix the ingredients until just combined. Divide the mixture into 8 equal portions. Roll each portion into a ball and gently pat each ball into a patty about ½ inch (1 cm) thick. Sandwich 1 slice of provolone between 2 patties. Crimp the edges with your fingers to encase the cheese. Press your thumb into the center of each patty to make a large dimple.

Arrange the patties on the grate over direct heat. Grill, undisturbed, for 4 minutes. Flip the patties and grill for 3 to 4 minutes more, until an instant-read thermometer inserted into the center of the meat reaches 160°F (71°C).

Arrange the ciabatta, cut-side down, on the grate over direct heat. Grill until lightly browned and crisp, 30 seconds to 1 minute. Transfer the bottom buns to a sheet pan. Turn the top buns over and grill for 30 seconds to 1 minute, until toasted.

To assemble the burgers, slather a layer of basil mustard on the bottom half of each ciabatta bun. Add a patty and a few spoonfuls of giardiniera, and place the other half of the bun on top. Serve with more giardiniera on the side.

Homemade Giardiniera

Giardiniera is the Italian word for "from the garden," and the beauty of this pickled condiment is you can make it with whatever fresh vegetables (from your garden or otherwise) are at their peak. For my giardiniera, I like to use a rainbow of spring and summer vegetables such as baby squash, cauliflower, carrots, bell peppers, and cherry bomb peppers (which are mild like jalapeños). You can't really go wrong here, though you should try to avoid vegetables that can discolor the pickles (like red beets).

I like to use organic canola oil because it's flavorless and doesn't detract from the crisp tanginess of the pickles. It also won't solidify in the fridge, but you can use any neutral or mild-flavored oil in its place, such as sunflower or avocado oil, and let the giardiniera come to room temperature before serving.

3 cups (weight varies) chopped or sliced mixed vegetables

1 serrano pepper, thinly sliced

¼ cup (75 g) kosher salt

2 teaspoons minced fresh oregano

½ teaspoon peppercorns, cracked

1 garlic clove, thinly sliced

¾ cup (180 ml) canola oil

¾ cup (180 ml) distilled white vinegar

—

Makes 1 quart (about 900 g)

In a large bowl, combine the mixed vegetables and serrano. Sprinkle the salt over the vegetables, toss to combine, and cover with water by at least 1 inch (2.5 cm). Let the vegetables sit at room temperature for at least 6 hours, or overnight. Drain the vegetables and rinse thoroughly to remove excess salt.

In a quart-size (960 ml) jar with a lid, combine the oregano, cracked peppercorns, and garlic. Add the canola oil and vinegar. Seal the jar and shake well until blended.

Pack the vegetables into the jar. With the back of a spoon, tamp down to submerge them in the brine. Re-cover the jar and refrigerate the giardiniera for 2 to 3 days before serving. (It only gets better as it ages!) Giardiniera will keep, refrigerated, for up to 3 months.

Coal-Blistered Shishito Peppers

Shishito peppers are like the Russian roulette of the food world—mostly mild in flavor, but, every few peppers, you might bite into one that sets your taste buds on fire! Along with their Spanish counterpart, Padrón peppers, shishitos are ideal for ember grilling because their thin skins mean they cook quickly and require no peeling. They make an easy and addictive appetizer while you prep the main course or a quick side dish after you take the meat off the coals.

1 pound (454 g) shishito peppers

4 teaspoons (20 ml) soy sauce

2 teaspoons toasted sesame oil

Kosher salt

—

Makes 4 servings

Prepare a hot single-level fire in a fire pit (see page 10). Spread the coals into a flat, uniform bed at least 2 inches (5 cm) deep. Briefly fan them with a rolled-up newspaper to disperse excess ash.

Arrange the peppers directly on the coals. Grill until charred all over, 3 to 4 minutes, turning frequently. Transfer the peppers to a sheet pan.

Drizzle with the soy sauce and sesame oil and toss to coat. Serve with a sprinkle of salt on top.

Seared Rib-Eye Steaks with Herbed Board Sauce

Of all the cuts of steak out there, rib eyes are among my favorite for their beautiful marbling and rich flavor. Slicing through buttery ribbons of fat on a rib eye just off the grill is almost as good as taking that first bite! And those buttery juices are the key to the simple herbed sauce, which you whip together on the same cutting board that you slice the steaks.

Essentially amped-up pan drippings, the fresh and earthy "board sauce" adds a depth of flavor to the steaks without overpowering them. You can use any mixture of herbs; try oregano, rosemary, basil, mint, or tarragon, depending on what you're serving on the side.

FOR THE SAUCE

1 shallot, sliced

½ cup (30 g) packed fresh parsley

2 tablespoons (6 g) snipped fresh chives

4 thyme sprigs, leaves stripped

2 garlic cloves, sliced

Kosher salt

Ground black pepper

Olive oil, for drizzling

FOR THE STEAKS

2 (1-pound, or 454 g, 1- to 1½-inch-, or 2 to 3.5 cm, thick) rib-eye steaks

Kosher salt

Ground black pepper

—
Makes 4 servings

Prepare a hot two-zone fire in a fire pit (see page 10) with a grill grate over the coals.

TO MAKE THE SAUCE: In the center of a large cutting board, mound the shallot, parsley, chives, thyme leaves, and garlic. Finely chop them together, using your knife to scrape and combine to meld the flavors. Sprinkle with a generous pinch of salt and pepper. Drizzle with olive oil and stir the pile of aromatics and herbs with the tip of your knife. Set aside until needed.

TO MAKE THE STEAKS: Generously season the steaks on both sides with salt and pepper. Arrange the steaks over direct heat. Grill, undisturbed, for 4 to 5 minutes. Keep an eye on the steaks, as the fat dripping off may cause flare-ups. Be prepared to move them to the cooler side of the grill if needed. Once the flames die down, move the steaks back over direct heat to finish cooking.

Flip the steaks and grill for 4 to 5 minutes more, until an instant-read thermometer inserted into the thickest part of the meat reaches 125°F (52°C) for medium-rare.

TO FINISH THE SAUCE: Transfer the steaks to the cutting board and place them on top of the aromatics and herbs. Let rest for 5 minutes to let the heat intensify the flavors. Slice the steak against the grain. Using tongs, toss the steaks with the herbed sauce. Divide into equal portions and serve.

Chapter 4

Feasting ... with Foil Packs

Foil packets have gone beyond the humble hobo packs of Boy Scout fame. Often lumped together with leftovers and relegated to camping food, they are so much more than appearances let on. They're mini ovens, steamers, serving bowls, and, yes, even a good way to get out of doing dishes. Crumple them up and you're done!

Despite the primitive package, there's an element of drama to cooking in a foil pack: You pile in the food, wrap it all up, put it on the fire, and hope for the best. You hear it spit and sizzle, but you won't know how it turns out until you peel it apart. The steam billows out, the smells fill your nose, and tucked inside the foil is an elegant self-contained meal—just add a fork.

Foil Pack 101

Foil packs are nearly foolproof in their simplicity, and the learning curve is as short as these three little tips.

Oil it: A thin layer of oil keeps food from sticking to the foil. I always start with a fine mist on the surface I'm working on, even if my ingredients are well sauced or well buttered. And contrary to what you may have heard, neither side of the foil (shiny or dull) makes a difference in how heat reflective or heatproof it is.

Grill it: You can certainly set your foil packs right on the coals, but I prefer using a grill grate so I have more control over temperature. I can dial down or turn up the heat as little or as much as I need, and I don't have to worry about losing my food to the fire if I accidentally put a hole in the foil.

Rotate it: With varying levels of heat coming at it from every which way, a foil pack is bound to cook unevenly if it sits in one spot. Rotate your packs every few minutes, and even shuffle them around the grill to account for hot spots and cool spots.

Perfecting the Foil Pack

The perfect foil pack begins with a roll of heavy-duty aluminum foil and a can of olive oil cooking spray.

Step 1: Measure a large sheet of foil and lightly mist the surface with cooking spray.

Step 2: Mound the food in the center of the foil. If the ingredients are especially runny, fold the edges up slightly to form a small lip to contain the liquid.

Step 3: Bring the two longer sides together and fold the edges over twice.

Step 4: Fold each short end over twice to seal the foil packet, leaving room inside for steam to circulate.

Use a pair of tongs or a spatula to maneuver your foil packs around the grill. Always be careful when opening, as the foil pack will be full of hot steam.

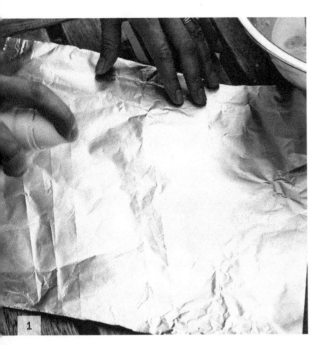

Foil Pack French Dip

Great for camping or casual meals at home, this nontraditional French dip is a fun pull-apart sandwich that comes together quickly, thanks to a couple of shortcuts: roast beef from the deli and a quick "au jus" made from butter. We might not have a homemade roast or a pan full of drippings, but we definitely aren't short on flavor here. Keep in mind the au jus will only be as good as your beef broth, so it's worth using a well-seasoned homemade broth or seeking out quality bone broth from a butcher shop.

Olive oil cooking spray, for preparing the aluminum foil

FOR THE AU JUS

4 tablespoons (½ stick, or 56 g) butter

1 tablespoon (8 g) all-purpose flour

2 cups (480 ml) well-seasoned beef broth

½ teaspoon Worcestershire sauce

Kosher salt

Ground black pepper

FOR THE SANDWICHES

8 tablespoons (1 stick, or 112 g) butter, at room temperature

1 tablespoon (4 g) minced fresh parsley

1 teaspoon Worcestershire sauce

1 teaspoon garlic powder

1 teaspoon onion powder

½ teaspoon ground black pepper

1 (1-pound, or 454 g) loaf French bread (about 16 inches, or 40 cm, long), halved widthwise so you have 2 (8-inch, or 20 cm) loaves

Dijon mustard, for spreading

12 slices provolone cheese

1 pound (454 g) thinly sliced deli roast beef

—

Makes 6 servings

Prepare a medium-hot two-zone fire in a charcoal grill (see page 10) with a grill grate over the coals.

Measure two sheets of heavy-duty aluminum foil (at least 18 inches, or 45 cm, long) and mist the surface of each sheet with cooking spray. Set aside until needed.

TO MAKE THE AU JUS: On the stovetop, in a medium saucepan over medium heat, melt the butter. Whisk the flour into the butter and cook, whisking frequently, until the flour is incorporated and the mixture thickens, 2 to 3 minutes.

Add the broth and Worcestershire and whisk to combine. Increase the heat and bring the mixture to a boil. Boil the au jus until it thickens slightly. Season to taste with salt and pepper. Keep warm until ready to use.

TO MAKE THE SANDWICHES: In a small bowl, using a fork, mash the butter, parsley, Worcestershire, garlic powder, onion powder, and pepper until well combined.

Cut even slits about ½ inch (1 cm) apart in each loaf, stopping just before you slice through the bottom so the slices hold together. You should have 12 equal "slices" of bread per loaf.

Spread a thin layer of the butter mixture on one side of every other slice. Spread a thin layer of Dijon on the opposite side of each buttered slice. Starting at the end of each loaf, tuck 1 slice of provolone and 2 slices of roast beef between the buttered and Dijon sides, so when the bread is pulled apart when serving they will become individual sandwiches.

Place a loaf in the center of each prepared foil sheet and lightly coat the tops and sides of the bread with the remaining butter mixture. Fold and seal the foil into packets (see page 56).

Place the foil packets on the grate over direct heat. Grill for 5 to 10 minutes, turning frequently, until the bread is toasted and the cheese is melted. If you'd like to add a bit more crispness, move the foil packs over indirect heat, open the packs to expose the top and sides of each loaf, and close the grill lid. Continue grilling for about 5 minutes more, until the bread is golden brown all the way through.

Serve the French dips family style with au jus on the side and let your guests pull apart their own sandwiches.

HOT TIP

If you plan to put leftover rib roast in these sandwiches, use the luscious pan drippings from your roast in place of the butter to make the au jus that much better!

Sweet Potatoes with Sriracha-Maple Glaze

Sweet potatoes and maple syrup are no strangers, but this recipe marries the predictable pairing with sriracha for a balanced blend of sweet and spicy in every bite. The silky sweet potatoes have a tendency to soak up all the glaze the longer they sit, so I recommend tossing them with the sriracha and maple syrup right before serving for the brightest punch of flavor.

Olive oil cooking spray, for preparing the aluminum foil

3 sweet potatoes (about 1½ pounds, or 681 g), cut into 1-inch (2.5 cm) chunks

Kosher salt

2 tablespoons (28 g) butter, cut into small pats

2 tablespoons (30 ml) maple syrup

2 teaspoons sriracha

⅓ cup (37 g) chopped walnuts

—

Makes 4 servings

Prepare a medium-hot single-level fire in a charcoal grill or fire pit (see page 10) with a grill grate over the coals.

Measure two sheets of heavy-duty aluminum foil (at least 16 inches, or 40 cm, long) and lightly spray the surface with cooking spray.

Divide the sweet potatoes between the two prepared sheets, piling them in the center. Mist the sweet potatoes with cooking spray, season with salt, and scatter the butter over the top. Fold and seal the foil into packets (see page 56).

Place the packets on the grate. Grill for 20 to 25 minutes, until the sweet potatoes are tender, rotating the packets every 5 to 10 minutes for even cooking.

Meanwhile, in a small bowl, stir together the maple syrup and sriracha until combined.

Transfer the foil packets to a sheet pan and use caution when opening, as they will be full of steam. Drizzle the maple syrup mixture over the sweet potatoes, sprinkle with the walnuts, and gently toss to coat.

HOT TIP

There's no need to peel sweet potatoes! The skins are edible, are full of nutrients, and add subtle texture. Simply scrub them with a vegetable brush under running water to make sure they're clean before cooking.

Potato and Prosciutto Packets

Whether you're looking for a simple side dish to serve with your main course or a potluck item you can take to a tailgate, foil-packet potatoes are always a crowd-pleaser. They're quick to throw together and tough to mess up, as long as you give them enough time on the grill to turn fluffy and velvety. In this recipe, Yukon gold potatoes get gussied up with creamy goat cheese and salty prosciutto, a sublime combination that goes well with almost any dish.

2 pounds (908 g) Yukon gold potatoes, cut into ¼-inch (0.6 cm) slices

1 tablespoon (15 ml) olive oil

1 tablespoon (2 g) minced fresh rosemary

Kosher salt

Ground black pepper

Olive oil cooking spray, for preparing the aluminum foil

4 thin slices prosciutto

4 ounces (115 g) goat cheese

—

Makes 4 servings

Prepare a hot single-level fire in a fire pit or charcoal grill (see page 10) with a grill grate over the coals.

In a large bowl, toss the potatoes with the olive oil, rosemary, and a few pinches of salt and pepper to evenly coat.

Measure four sheets of heavy-duty aluminum foil (at least 14 inches, or 35 cm, long) and spritz the surface of each sheet with cooking spray.

Mound an equal portion of potatoes in the center of each prepared foil sheet. Drape 1 slice of prosciutto over each mound. Top each with a few dollops of goat cheese and fold and seal the foil into packets (see page 56).

Place the packets on the grate. Grill for about 35 minutes, rotating every 10 minutes for even cooking. Transfer the foil packets to a sheet pan and use caution when opening, as they will be full of steam. The potatoes are done when the flesh is easily pierced with a fork.

Garlicky Salmon

Garlic lovers, this recipe is for you! And it's so easy to pull off you can pick up a salmon on your way home and prepare it in a few minutes with a handful of pantry staples. I love serving a large platter of salmon like this alongside grilled vegetables for a well-rounded meal that requires little hands-on time and even fewer dishes to do. It's a weeknight win all around!

2 tablespoons (28 g) butter

6 garlic cloves, chopped

2 tablespoons (30 ml) dry white wine

1 tablespoon (15 ml) fresh lemon juice

Olive oil cooking spray, for preparing the aluminum foil

1 (1½- to 2-pound, or 681 to 908 g) side of salmon

Kosher salt

Ground black pepper

1 lemon, halved crosswise

Finely chopped fresh parsley, for garnishing

—

Makes 4 servings

Prepare a medium-hot single-level fire in a fire pit or charcoal grill (see page 10) with a grill grate over the coals.

On the stovetop, in a small saucepan over medium heat, melt the butter. Add the garlic. Cook until fragrant, 1 to 2 minutes. Stir in the white wine and lemon juice. Bring the sauce to a simmer, cook for 1 minute, and remove from the heat.

Measure a sheet of heavy-duty aluminum foil (at least 18 inches, or 45 cm, long, or long enough to wrap the salmon) and lightly spritz the surface with cooking spray.

Pat the salmon dry with paper towels and place it in the center of the prepared foil sheet. Pour the sauce evenly over the top and season with salt and pepper. Fold and seal the foil into a packet (see page 56).

Place the packet on the grate. Grill for 10 to 12 minutes, rotating the packet every 3 to 5 minutes for even cooking. (Depending on the thickness of your salmon, cooking time may vary by a few minutes.) Transfer the foil packet to a sheet pan and use caution when opening, as it will be full of steam. The salmon is done when the flesh flakes easily with a fork and an instant-read thermometer inserted into the thickest part of the flesh registers 120°F to 125°F (49°C to 52°C).

Lightly mist the lemon halves with cooking spray and place them, cut-side down, on the grate. Grill for about 5 minutes, until the edges are charred. Squeeze the lemons over the salmon and garnish with a sprinkle of parsley. Serve the salmon family style or cut it into individual portions for plating.

Spicy Smoked Sausage, Snap Beans, and Potatoes

When I make foil packets, it's usually to save time and have an easy side dish ready while the main event is on the grill. But this recipe is so flavorful and filling on its own it can be the main event! I like to make a few of these packets to bring camping or tailgating, too—they hold well and travel well, and my favorite Cajun Creole spice blend (an intermingling of fiery, savory, and earthy flavors) keeps them from being boring.

1 pound (454 g) smoked andouille sausage, cut into ½-inch (1 cm) slices

1 pound (454 g) baby potatoes, quartered

8 ounces (225 g) snap beans, trimmed and halved

8 ounces (225 g) cremini mushrooms, quartered

1 yellow onion, chopped

2 tablespoons (30 ml) olive oil

4 teaspoons (10 g) Cajun Creole Spice Blend (recipe follows)

Olive oil cooking spray, for preparing the aluminum foil

4 tablespoons (½ stick, or 56 g) butter, cut into small pats

Handful chopped fresh parsley, for garnishing

—
Makes 4 servings

Prepare a hot single-level fire in a fire pit or charcoal grill (see page 10) with a grill grate over the coals.

In a large bowl, combine the sausage, potatoes, snap beans, mushrooms, and onion. Drizzle with the olive oil and sprinkle the spice blend over. Toss to coat.

Measure four sheets of heavy-duty aluminum foil (at least 14 inches, or 35 cm, long) and mist the surface of each sheet with cooking spray.

Evenly divide the sausage-vegetable mixture among the prepared foil sheets, heaping them into a mound in the center. Scatter a few pats of butter over each mound and fold and seal the foil into packets (see page 56).

Place the packets on the grate. Grill for about 35 minutes, rotating the packets every 10 minutes for even cooking. Transfer the foil packets to a sheet pan and use caution when opening, as they will be full of steam. The vegetables are done when the potatoes are easily pierced with a fork.

Garnish each packet with a sprinkle of parsley before serving.

HOT TIP

To ensure the potatoes cook all the way through, halve or quarter them into chunks no larger than ½ inch (1 cm).

Cajun Creole Spice Blend

Inspired by the mosaic of French, Spanish, African, and Caribbean cultures that flourishes in New Orleans, this seasoning blend imparts a robust smoky flavor, mild kick, and deep color to dishes. It's also featured in my Juicy Jumbo Creole Shrimp (page 77).

2 tablespoons (17 g) paprika

1 tablespoon (18 g)
kosher salt

1 tablespoon (9 g) garlic powder

1 tablespoon (7 g) onion powder

2 teaspoons dried oregano

2 teaspoons dried basil

2 teaspoons dried thyme

1 teaspoon cayenne pepper

1 teaspoon ground
black pepper

1 teaspoon ground white pepper

Makes ½ cup (60 g)

In a small bowl, stir together all the ingredients. Transfer the spice blend to an airtight lidded container and store in a cool, dark, dry place until needed. The spice blend will keep for up to 6 months, after which it will start to lose potency.

Garlic Butter Gnocchi and Mushrooms

This hearty recipe is simple enough to prepare and stow for a weeknight meal, yet full of flavor and texture thanks to the plump, velvety gnocchi, the silky umami-rich mushrooms, and the garlicky, buttery broth they steam in. I like to use packaged Parmesan gnocchi for an added layer of flavor, but there's no reason you couldn't finish this dish with a sprinkle of freshly grated Parmesan cheese. To take it up a notch, try it with a medley of wild mushrooms like chanterelle, morel, and maitake.

20 ounces (569 g) fresh gnocchi

12 ounces (340 g) cremini mushrooms, quartered

Olive oil, for drizzling

4 garlic cloves, minced

1 teaspoon kosher salt

½ teaspoon red pepper flakes

¼ teaspoon ground black pepper

Olive oil cooking spray, for preparing the aluminum foil

1 cup (240 ml) chicken broth, or ½ cup (120 ml) chicken broth and ½ cup (120 ml) dry white wine

4 tablespoons (½ stick, or 56 g) butter, cut into pats

Finely chopped fresh parsley, for garnishing

—
Makes 4 servings

Prepare a hot single-level fire in a fire pit or charcoal grill (see page 10) with a grill grate over the coals.

In a large bowl, combine the gnocchi and mushrooms. Generously drizzle with olive oil. Add the garlic, salt, red pepper flakes, and black pepper and toss until coated.

Measure four sheets of heavy-duty aluminum foil (at least 14 inches, or 35 cm, long) and spritz the surface of each sheet with cooking spray.

Pile an equal portion of the gnocchi and mushroom mixture in the center of each prepared foil sheet. Fold all four sides up on each sheet (as if you were making a bowl) and pour ¼ cup (60 ml) of chicken broth into each packet. Scatter a few pats of butter over the top of each and fold and seal the foil into packets (see page 56).

Place the packets on the grate. Grill for about 15 minutes, rotating every 5 minutes for even cooking. Transfer the foil packets to a sheet pan and use caution when opening, as they will be full of steam.

Glazed Cinnamon-Sugar Peaches

Add this to your list of no-fail, no-fuss desserts by the fire: It's lovely on its own, with bits of caramelized sugar and a touch of cinnamon, but even better when paired with a scoop of vanilla ice cream and, perhaps, a slice of grilled pound cake. It also holds well, so you can grill it right after your main course to take advantage of the initial heat. Come dessert time, simply reheat the peaches in their foil packets over the last of the coals.

Olive oil cooking spray, for preparing the aluminum foil

4 peaches, pitted and quartered

3 tablespoons (36 g) packed light brown sugar

¼ teaspoon ground cinnamon

2 tablespoons (28 g) butter, cut into small pats

—

Makes 4 to 8 servings

Prepare a medium-hot single-level fire in a fire pit or charcoal grill (see page 10) with a grill grate over the coals.

Measure four sheets of heavy-duty aluminum foil (at least 16 inches, or 40 cm, long) and mist the surface with cooking spray.

Divide the peaches among the foil, placing them in the center of each prepared foil sheet, and sprinkle the brown sugar and cinnamon over them. Dot the peaches with the butter and fold and seal the foil into packets (see page 56).

Place the packets on the grate. Grill for 10 to 12 minutes, rotating every 3 minutes for even cooking. Transfer the foil packets to a sheet pan and use caution when opening, as they will be full of steam.

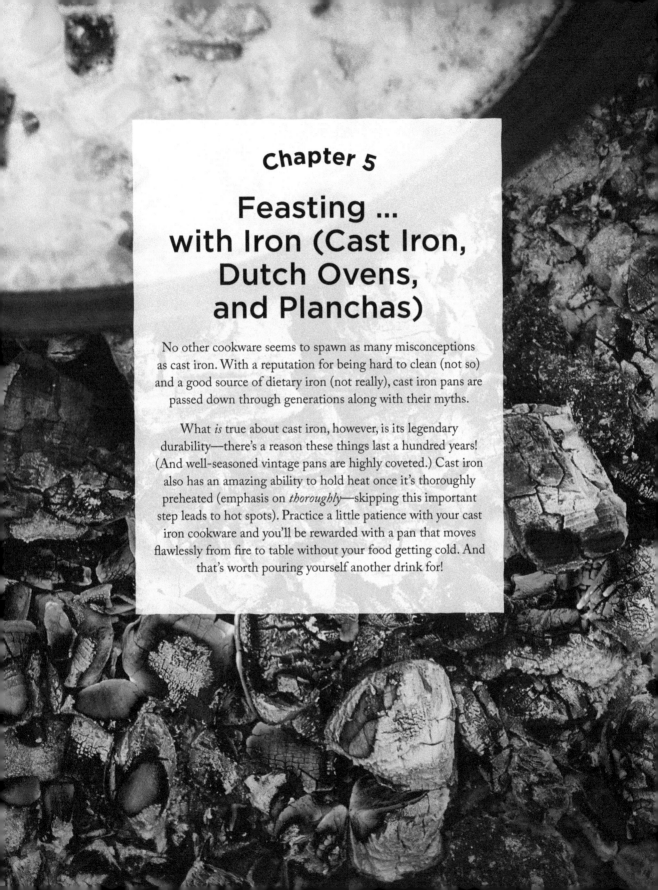

Chapter 5

Feasting ... with Iron (Cast Iron, Dutch Ovens, and Planchas)

No other cookware seems to spawn as many misconceptions as cast iron. With a reputation for being hard to clean (not so) and a good source of dietary iron (not really), cast iron pans are passed down through generations along with their myths.

What *is* true about cast iron, however, is its legendary durability—there's a reason these things last a hundred years! (And well-seasoned vintage pans are highly coveted.) Cast iron also has an amazing ability to hold heat once it's thoroughly preheated (emphasis on *thoroughly*—skipping this important step leads to hot spots). Practice a little patience with your cast iron cookware and you'll be rewarded with a pan that moves flawlessly from fire to table without your food getting cold. And that's worth pouring yourself another drink for!

The Big Three of Cast Iron

Inexpensive and tough as nails, these versatile workhorses allow you to make any of the cast iron recipes in this book, as well as open your fire pit or grill to countless new meals you may not have thought were possible over a fire.

12-inch (30 cm) skillet: A good all-around size, this pan can cook up a meal for four people. I highly recommend buying an ovenproof lid for it, or repurposing an ovenproof lid from another pan that fits it well.

8-quart (7.7 L) Dutch oven: Some Dutch ovens are designed for stovetop and oven use, but the one you want is the classic camping version with three feet and a flanged lid. These features allow you to place coals under and on top of the Dutch oven to heat it.

15 x 17-inch (37.5 x 43 cm) plancha: Essentially a griddle, planchas are popular in Spain and many other parts of the world, where the fiery style of cooking involves grilling food on a hot metal slab. I prefer a plancha with a shallow rim, as it helps corral the ingredients when I'm turning and tossing them.

You will also need vegetable oil for seasoning (I prefer canola oil) and a plastic pan scraper for cleaning.

Useful accessories to have for Dutch oven cooking include a lid lifter, a wire rack or other heatproof landing zone for the lid, and a whisk broom for sweeping coals and ash off the lid.

Seasoning Your Cast Iron

Modern cast iron cookware comes preseasoned from the factory, but it doesn't hurt to season again when you bring the cookware home. Rinse and dry the cookware and heat it on the stovetop until smoking. Apply a very thin layer of oil to the cast iron and rub it in thoroughly with a paper towel (across the bottom, up and down the sides, and along the handle). Buff it out with a clean towel and turn off the heat. Let the cast iron cool completely, then reheat and repeat the process several times to build up the seasoning.

Alternatively, season your cookware in the oven. Rinse, dry, oil, and buff the cast iron inside and out, and set it upside down in a cold oven. Place a large sheet of foil underneath to catch any drips. Heat the oven to 450°F (230°C). Bake for 1 hour, turn off the oven, and let the cookware cool inside. Repeat the process as many times as needed until the cast iron achieves a smooth, subtle, evenly dark sheen. If it feels sticky or looks blotchy after seasoning, it's likely you used too much oil. Simply scrub it off, wash with soap, and try again.

Properly seasoned cookware is more durable than most people think, so it's fine to use metal utensils, stainless steel scrubbers, and scouring pads on your cast iron without fear of removing the seasoning.

Cleaning and Caring for Cast Iron

There's a common misconception you should never wash your cast iron cookware, but a mild dishwashing soap is harmless to the seasoning and actually helpful for getting all the gunk off the surface (gunk such as old grease, rancid oil, and other undesirables that linger on unwashed cookware).

The important thing to remember is *never put cold water on hot cast iron*. The thermal shock could cause the cast iron to crack.

For safe and easy cleaning, wait until the cast iron has cooled enough to handle. Scrape off any food remnants and wash your cookware with a dab of soap and a dish scrubber. You can also sprinkle a handful of kosher salt on the surface and work it in with your brush for extra scrubbing power. If any stubborn spots remain, boil some water in the cookware until the burnt-on bits soften and release. Rinse well and dry with a towel. Set the cookware on the stovetop over medium-low heat until the cast iron is completely dry. Season with a light layer of oil, wipe the excess oil with a clean towel, remove from the heat, and let cool.

Store your cast iron in a clean, dry place to discourage rust. Use it regularly to improve the seasoning and never leave it soaking in water. Avoid cooking with very acidic foods (such as citrus, wine, and tomato sauce) until the cast iron is well seasoned.

If your cookware has a few rust spots, you can soak it in a 50/50 solution of distilled white vinegar and water for at least 1 hour (up to 6 hours) until the rust dissolves. If your cookware is severely rusted, however, you can use steel wool to strip the seasoning and scrape it down to bare iron before re-seasoning in the oven.

Cooking with a Dutch Oven

Dutch ovens are made for the volatility of live-fire cooking, as they're very forgiving in less-than-ideal conditions. Used as ovens or pots, they adapt to a wide range of recipes and require no special space of their own. You can simply set a galvanized steel oil pan on a heatproof surface and spread your coals in it, or place a double layer of heavy-duty aluminum foil on dirt to start cooking.

Arranging the Coals

Longtime standards for controlling temperature in a Dutch oven involve setting specific numbers of coals below the oven and on the lid. These formulas work well when using charcoal briquettes, but with hardwood and hardwood lump charcoal—which are not consistently sized—it's difficult to go by the coal-counting method. An easier way to regulate temperature for Dutch oven cooking is to use the "ring method."

In this book, I specify temperature as 1 ring, 1½ rings, 2 rings, or a full spread.

- **1 ring:** A circle of coals with all the coals touching. The outside edge of the circle is lined up with the outside edge of the Dutch oven, top or bottom.

- **1½ rings:** The same as 1 ring with an additional ½ ring inside, touching the first ring. A ½ ring is a circle of coals with every other coal taken out.

- **2 rings:** A second ring of coals is placed inside the first ring, with both rings touching.

- **Full spread:** The coals are spread out in a single even layer with all coals touching.

Using a combination of rings for top and bottom heating allows you to reach the approximate temperature needed for baking, boiling, and browning. For baking, I always start with 1 ring on the bottom as a "burner," and then place either 1½ rings on top for medium heat (350°F to 375°F, or 180°C to 190°C) or 2 rings on top for high heat (400°F to 425°F, or 200°C to 220°C). For searing, frying, or boiling, I concentrate all the heat on the bottom with a full spread of coals.

Using a pair of tongs or a grill rake, break apart odd-shape or oversize coals into roughly the same size so they're easier to manage. Remember that different types of wood and charcoal, outside air temperature, wind, sun, and shade can all affect heat output, so trust your senses and adjust the rings as needed to work with your conditions. The best way to master temperature control on a Dutch oven is to stay loyal to the same brand of lump charcoal or the same type of wood. With practice, you'll learn how hot a ring of coals makes your oven and how much you need each time you cook.

Coals also burn out at different rates and develop hot spots. It's helpful to rotate the Dutch oven and/or lid 180 degrees every 20 minutes or so while your food cooks to encourage even heating. This is also a good time to supplement or replenish the coals to maintain temperature.

Spatchcocked Chicken Under a Skillet

I'll admit it, "spatchcock" is simply a fun word to say! Linguistics aside, it's also the best way to cook a whole bird if you want to attain the Holy Grail of grilled chicken—crispy skin, juicy breasts, and tender thighs all at the same time. Spatchcocking involves butterflying a whole chicken by removing the backbone (which is easier than it sounds, and much easier after your first time) so the meat lies flat and cooks more evenly. The classic Italian method (*pollo al mattone*) uses bricks to weight the chicken down for an all-over char on the skin; in this recipe, I use what I always have around—a heavy cast iron skillet.

You can try any combination of herbs in this recipe; in fact, I sometimes call it "fresh-from-the-garden marinade" (or perhaps more often, "leftover-herbs-in-the-back-of-the-fridge marinade") because I've never gone wrong with any handful of fresh, fragrant herbs. My favorites are thyme, oregano, rosemary, parsley, and cilantro—sometimes just a few, and sometimes all at once.

1 (4-pound, or 1.8 kg) whole chicken, giblets removed, patted dry with paper towels

½ cup (120 ml) olive oil

Zest and juice of 1 lemon

⅓ cup (weight varies) mixed minced fresh herbs

2 garlic cloves, minced

¼ teaspoon red pepper flakes

Kosher salt

Ground black pepper

1 lemon, halved crosswise

—
Makes 4 servings

To spatchcock the chicken:

1. Place the chicken, breast-side down, on a cutting board so the chicken's back is facing up. Using heavy-duty kitchen or poultry shears, start at the cavity next to the thigh and cut along one side of the backbone to the neck.

2. Cut along the other side of the backbone.

3. Completely remove the backbone (discard it or save it for stock).

4. Flip the chicken, breast-side up, and firmly flatten it with the palm of your hand to crack the breastbone.

5. Cut off the wing tips and discard (or save for stock).

In a small bowl, whisk the olive oil, lemon zest, lemon juice, herbs, garlic, and red pepper flakes until combined. Place the chicken in a baking dish and pour the marinade over the chicken. Rub the marinade all over the skin until evenly coated. Cover and refrigerate for at least 2 hours, or overnight.

Prepare a medium-hot two-zone fire in a charcoal grill (see page 10) with a grill grate over the coals. Cover the outside bottom of a cast iron skillet with foil. Set aside until ready to use.

continued

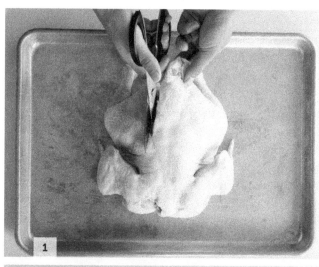

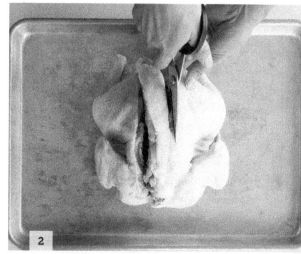

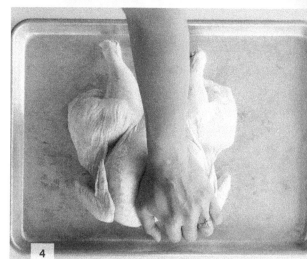

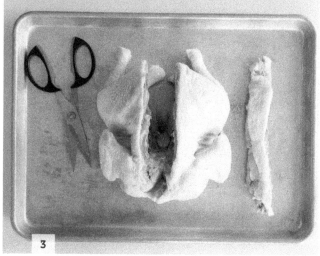

Lift the chicken out of the marinade and let the excess oil drip off. Liberally season the chicken with salt and pepper. Place the chicken, skin-side down, on the grate over direct heat with the breasts facing the cooler side of the grill. Place the prepared skillet on top of the chicken to weight it down and close the grill lid. Grill for 10 to 15 minutes, until the skin is brown and crisp.

Remove the skillet, flip the chicken, and move it over indirect heat with the legs facing the hotter side of the grill. Close the grill lid. Grill for 20 to 30 minutes, until an instant-read thermometer inserted into the thickest part of the breast reads 160°F (71°C). (For extra crispy skin, you can flip it one more time, skin-side down, over direct heat for a few minutes more.) Transfer the chicken to a cutting board and let rest for 10 minutes.

Place the lemon halves, cut-side down, on the grill over direct heat. Grill for about 5 minutes, until the edges are charred.

Carve and serve the chicken with a squeeze of charred lemon on top.

Not Just a Fun Word to Say . . .

Where did the term *spatchcock* come from? Though up for debate, one theory from the folks at *Oxford English Dictionary* is the word has Irish origins, and is an abbreviation of "dispatch cock," a phrase referring to fowl "split open and grilled after being killed, plucked, and dressed in a summary fashion."

Juicy Jumbo Creole Shrimp

Get your napkins ready, because this dish is best eaten with your fingers from start to finish! Luscious shrimp in the shell are simmered in a buttery, spicy, tomato-y broth that's good enough to eat on its own. And you certainly can—but I love having a loaf of French bread on hand to soak up all the juices. For variation, serve it over rice or noodles. I don't recommend taking a shortcut with peeled shrimp here, as the shells add a nice depth of flavor to the dipping broth.

2 cups (480 ml) seafood stock

1 cup (240 ml) pilsner or pale lager

3 tablespoons (48 g) tomato paste

2 tablespoons (15 g) Cajun Creole Spice Blend (page 64)

Juice of 1 lemon

1 tablespoon (15 ml) Worcestershire sauce

1 tablespoon (15 ml) Louisiana-style hot sauce, plus more as needed

1 teaspoon ground black pepper

2 garlic cloves, minced

2 pounds (908 g) jumbo shrimp, tail-on and unpeeled

8 tablespoons (1 stick, or 112 g) butter, cut into small cubes

Kosher salt

Crusty French bread, for serving

—
Makes 4 servings

Prepare a hot single-level fire in a fire pit or charcoal grill (see page 10) with a grill grate over the coals. Place a well-seasoned cast iron skillet on the grate and preheat for at least 5 minutes.

In the hot skillet, combine the seafood stock, pilsner, tomato paste, Cajun Creole spice blend, lemon juice, Worcestershire sauce, hot sauce, pepper, and garlic. Stir to combine. Cover the skillet with a lid and bring the ingredients to a simmer. Simmer for about 15 minutes, until the sauce is fragrant and well blended.

Add the shrimp and stir to coat with the sauce. Cook for 5 to 10 minutes, until the shrimp are opaque and just cooked through, stirring occasionally.

Remove the skillet from the heat. Scatter the butter over the shrimp and stir to melt the cubes into the sauce. Taste and season with salt or add more hot sauce, as desired. Serve with crusty bread to sop up all the broth.

HOT TIP

Make the Cajun Creole Spice Blend (page 64) a staple in your spice pantry! You can also use it in my Spicy Smoked Sausage, Snap Beans, and Potatoes (page 63).

Griddled French Toast Rolls with Blueberries and Cream

I love finding interesting new ways to make and serve old favorites, like French toast. This variation uses a loaf of sandwich bread—just plain ol' white bread, and fresh bread at that—to turn the traditional toast into French toast roll-ups stuffed with blueberry preserves. The whole batch cooks at once on a plancha so everyone can enjoy them while they're hot and toasty. (That's a real sticking point for me when it comes to making breakfast items such as French toast and pancakes—be sure to check out my Buttermilk Pancakes with Maple, Mascarpone, and Berries on page 28, if you feel the same way!)

Don't skimp on the velvety whipped cream by using store-bought. The crème fraîche adds just the right amount of tang to cut through the sweetness of the French toast and it gives the cream extra body and smoothness, almost like eating clouds.

FOR THE WHIPPED CREAM

¼ cup (56 g) crème fraîche

2 tablespoons (15 g) confectioners' sugar

1 cup (240 ml) heavy cream

FOR THE FRENCH TOAST

2 large eggs, beaten

⅓ cup (80 ml) milk

2 tablespoons (25 g) granulated sugar

½ teaspoon ground cinnamon

¼ teaspoon kosher salt

16 slices soft white sandwich bread, crusts removed

Blueberry preserves, for spreading

2 tablespoons (28 g) butter

1½ cups (220 g) fresh blueberries

Maple syrup, for serving (optional)

—
Makes 4 servings

TO MAKE THE WHIPPED CREAM: At least 30 minutes before you plan to make the whipped cream, place a large deep bowl and large balloon whisk in the freezer to chill. You want to start with very cold tools and ingredients for successfully whipping the cream. Alternatively, if using a handheld electric mixer, stand mixer, or high-powered blender, there is no need to freeze the whisk or bowl.

In a small bowl, using a fork, mix together the crème fraîche and confectioners' sugar until combined.

In the chilled bowl, using the chilled whisk (or using an unchilled bowl with the handheld mixer, stand mixer, or blender on medium to medium-high speed) beat the heavy cream until stiff peaks form. Using a rubber spatula, gently fold the crème fraîche into the whipped cream until smooth and blended. Cover and refrigerate until ready to serve.

TO MAKE THE FRENCH TOAST: Prepare a medium single-level fire in a fire pit or charcoal grill (see page 10) with a grill grate over the coals.

In a medium bowl, whisk the eggs, milk, granulated sugar, cinnamon, and salt until well blended. Set aside until needed.

Using a rolling pin, roll out each slice of bread to ⅛ inch (0.3 cm) thickness. Spread a thin layer of blueberry preserves on each slice of bread and roll each tightly into a cylinder, up and away from you. Dip each roll into the egg mixture until lightly coated on all sides.

Place a well-seasoned plancha on the grate and preheat for at least 5 minutes.

On the plancha, melt the butter, spreading it around to evenly coat the surface. Arrange the rolls in a single layer on the plancha. Cook until all four sides are golden brown, 1 to 2 minutes per side.

Remove the whipped cream from the fridge and give it a few turns with a whisk.

Serve the French toast rolls with a dollop of whipped cream, a handful of fresh blueberries, and maple syrup for dipping (if desired).

Deconstructed BLT Salad

Lettuce is probably not the first thing that comes to mind when you think "grilling," but it's one of my favorite vegetables to put on the grill because the high heat transforms it from bland and boring to something much more interesting. (Brushing it with bacon fat doesn't hurt either.) If you're looking for a new take on salad for your next barbecue, this is it!

FOR THE DRESSING

¼ cup (60 g) mayonnaise

¼ cup (60 ml) buttermilk

3 tablespoons (45 ml) distilled white vinegar

2 tablespoons (6 g) minced fresh chives

Kosher salt

Ground black pepper

FOR THE SALAD

1 pound (454 g) tomatoes, cut into ½-inch (1 cm) wedges

Kosher salt

6 thick-cut bacon slices

6 (½-inch, or 1 cm) slices French bread

2 hearts of romaine lettuce, halved lengthwise, root end intact

Ground black pepper

—

Makes 6 to 8 servings

Prepare a medium-hot single-level fire in a fire pit or charcoal grill (see page 10) with a grill grate over the coals. Place a well-seasoned plancha on the grate and preheat for at least 5 minutes.

TO MAKE THE DRESSING: In a bowl large enough to hold the salad, whisk all the dressing ingredients until combined. Set aside.

TO MAKE THE SALAD: Season the tomatoes with salt and place them in a colander. Let drain while you grill the remaining ingredients.

Arrange the bacon on the plancha. Cook for 2 to 3 minutes per side, until browned and crisp. Transfer the bacon to paper towels to drain. Slice into ½-inch (1 cm) strips. Remove the plancha from the grill and reserve the bacon grease.

Lightly brush the bread with the bacon grease and arrange it on the grate. Grill for about 30 seconds per side, until toasted with good grill marks. Transfer the bread to a cutting board and cut into ½-inch (1 cm) chunks.

Lightly brush the lettuce with bacon grease and season with salt and pepper. Place the lettuce on the grate, cut-side down, and grill for about 2 minutes, until charred on the outside but still crisp and raw inside. Turn the lettuce over and grill until the outer leaves are slightly wilted, 1 to 2 minutes. Transfer the lettuce to a cutting board. Trim and discard the ends and slice the lettuce crosswise into ½-inch (1 cm) strips.

Add the bacon, bread, lettuce, and tomatoes to the bowl with the dressing. Immediately before serving, gently toss the salad until combined and evenly coated with dressing.

Lemon-Dill Salmon a la Plancha

On a plancha, these meaty salmon steaks sear in their own juices, concentrate all that zippy flavor from the lemon and dill dressing, and develop a mouthwatering crust without the downsides of cooking fish on a grill. (You know—the agony of burning, sticking, and leaving half the flesh on the grate.) The key to picture-perfect salmon is waiting for that crust to form; don't flip too early because, as the flesh turns crackly and golden brown, the fish will release easily from the plancha.

¼ cup (60 ml) olive oil

2 tablespoons (30 ml) dry white wine

2 tablespoons (8 g) minced fresh dill

2 tablespoons (30 ml) fresh lemon juice

Zest of 1 lemon

4 (8-ounce, or 225 g, 1½-inch, or 3.5 cm, -thick) salmon steaks

Kosher salt

Ground black pepper

1 lemon, thinly sliced

—

Makes 4 servings

Prepare a hot single-level fire in a charcoal grill (see page 10) with a grill grate over the coals. Place a well-seasoned plancha on the grate and preheat for at least 5 minutes.

In a small bowl, whisk the olive oil, wine, dill, lemon juice, and lemon zest. Set aside one-third of the sauce. Generously brush the remaining sauce on both sides of the salmon and season it with salt and pepper.

Arrange the salmon on the plancha and close the grill lid. Grill, undisturbed, for about 5 minutes. Turn the salmon over and re-close the grill lid. Grill for about 5 minutes more, until an instant-read thermometer inserted into the thickest part of the flesh reaches 120°F to 125°F (49°C to 52°C).

Arrange a few lemon slices on each serving plate and place the salmon on top. Add a heaping spoonful of the reserved lemon-dill sauce over each salmon before serving.

Grilled Pork Medallions with Cherry-Bourbon Sauce

Tenderloins are one of my favorite cuts of pork, and these medallions (just a frilly term for sliced tenderloin) stay true to their name, turning oh so tender and incredibly juicy on the grill. The key to not overcooking the meat is searing it over direct heat to get a good char, and finishing over indirect heat. A sweet and savory cherry sauce spiked with bourbon—which we cook right on the grill grate while the pork rests—makes this deceptively fancy meal seem like you put a lot more work into it than you actually did.

FOR THE PORK

2 (1-pound, or 454 g) pork tenderloins, trimmed of excess fat

Kosher salt

Ground black pepper

FOR THE SAUCE

4 tablespoons (½ stick, or 56 g) butter

½ shallot, finely chopped

1 pound (454 g) sweet cherries, pitted and halved

¼ cup (60 ml) bourbon

2 tablespoons (30 ml) balsamic vinegar

2 thyme sprigs, leaves stripped

—
Makes 4 servings

Prepare a medium-hot two-zone fire in a charcoal grill (see page 10) with a grill grate over the coals.

TO MAKE THE PORK: Liberally season the pork with salt and pepper. Place the pork on the grate over direct heat. Sear for about 2 minutes on all four sides, until evenly charred. Move the pork over indirect heat and close the grill lid. Grill for about 4 minutes on each of the wider sides, until an instant-read thermometer inserted into the center reaches 140°F (60°C). Transfer the pork to a cutting board, tent with aluminum foil, and let rest while you prepare the sauce.

TO MAKE THE SAUCE: Preheat a well-seasoned cast iron skillet on the grate over direct heat. Add the butter to melt. Stir in the shallot. Cook for about 2 minutes, until it starts to turns translucent. Add the cherries, bourbon, and vinegar. Cook for 5 to 7 minutes until the cherries are soft and the sauce is reduced to a thin syrup. Stir in the thyme leaves and remove the skillet from the heat.

Slice the pork and serve with a few spoonfuls of sauce on top.

Chapter 6

Feasting ...
with a Grill

You don't need an expensive grill with all the bells and
whistles to turn out great food. You just need a good cover
and functioning vents, two simple features that will help you
make a four-star meal with more control and better timing
than you'd typically get from a fire pit. By manipulating
airflow in a tighter environment, you can use your grill
for high-heat searing as well as slow roasting and baking.
Nearly anything you can cook on the stovetop or in the
oven, you can cook on the grill.

Start with a midrange model when buying your first grill,
and choose one that's a little larger than you think you need.
You don't always have to fill the whole box with coals, but
you'll be glad for the extra space.

Preparing Your Grill for Cooking

Start with the top and bottom dampers fully open. Remove the top (cooking) grate and light your charcoal (see page 9). Once the coals are ready and raked into your desired cooking zones (see page 10), replace the top grate, close the grill lid, and let the grate preheat for about 10 minutes. Adjust the dampers as needed to hit your target temperature.

Adjusting the Temperature of Your Grill

Fire is a fickle heat source but, on a grill, you can tame the flames with little effort once you learn to use the dampers (or vents).

The dampers control the amount of air that flows through the grill. Air is your friend when it comes to starting and maintaining a fire, so, by controlling the airflow, you control the heat.

The bottom damper brings oxygen to the fire. The top damper acts as a chimney, creating a draft that pulls heat and smoke out of your grill. Opening the dampers allows more air to enter, meaning more heat; closing the dampers means less air and less heat. Remember the cardinal rule of venting: **close to cool, open to heat**. Adjust the vents in tandem and give the fire time to react in order to reach its final temperature. Keep in mind that closing and opening the grill lid can affect the temperature gauge, so it's not always an accurate measure of heat.

It takes some practice to figure out the ideal damper settings for your grill but, in most circumstances, you can leave the top and bottom dampers partially open to maintain temperatures between 300°F and 500°F (150°C and 260°C). I typically leave my bottom damper in one position while I adjust the top damper; this method often gets me within 5°F to 10°F (2°C to 4°C) of the needed temperature.

If you still have charcoal remaining after a grill session, close the top and bottom dampers to choke the fire. You can save and use the unburned charcoal next time.

Caring for Your Grill

A little goes a long way when it comes to grill maintenance. Get into the habit of doing a few simple tasks each time you grill, and you'll save yourself a lot of elbow grease, time, and money at the end of the season.

Every grill session:

- Empty the ash catcher.

- Clean and oil the grate *before* and *after* you grill.

- If inclement weather is forecast, cover the grill with a waterproof cover or store it indoors.

Once every few months:

- Deep clean the grates and the inside and outside of your grill once a season to prevent buildup of soot and grease.

- Lubricate the dampers with WD-40 if they feel sticky.

Homemade Basil-Walnut Pesto

Fresh and earthy, this pesto leans toward the traditional side but uses rich, buttery walnuts in place of pine nuts. A squeeze of lemon at the end adds brightness.

2 cups (70 g) packed fresh basil

½ cup (50 g) grated Parmesan cheese

⅓ cup (50 g) walnuts

3 garlic cloves, peeled

½ teaspoon kosher salt

¼ to ⅓ cup (60 to 80 ml) olive oil

Squeeze of fresh lemon juice

—
Makes 1 cup (260 g)

In a food processor, combine the basil, cheese, walnuts, garlic, and salt. Pulse to combine, scraping down the sides of the bowl with a rubber spatula as needed. With the processor running on low speed, add the olive oil in a slow, steady stream until the mixture becomes a smooth, thin, spreadable paste. (If you are making pesto to use as a sauce or drizzle for other recipes, feel free to add up to ¼ cup [60 ml] more oil for a thinner consistency.)

Transfer the pesto to an airtight container and stir in a squeeze of lemon juice. Refrigerate for up to 1 week, or freeze for 6 to 9 months.

Homemade Pizza Dough

When you see how simple it is to make your own dough, you may never go back to buying prepared pizza dough or premade crusts from the store.

2 tablespoons (30 ml) olive oil, plus more for greasing

1 cup (240 ml) warm water (100°F to 110°F, or 38°C to 43°C)

1 teaspoon active dry yeast

1 teaspoon sugar

1 teaspoon kosher salt

½ teaspoon garlic powder

2½ cups (310 g) all-purpose flour

—
Makes 1 pound (enough for 2 pizzas)

Lightly grease a medium bowl with olive oil and set aside.

In another medium bowl, stir together the warm water, yeast, sugar, salt, and garlic powder until combined (the ingredients do not need to be fully dissolved). Add the olive oil and flour. Using a large sturdy spoon, mix until no dry pockets remain and a loose, shaggy dough forms.

Knead the dough by hand for 3 to 5 minutes, until it looks and feels smooth. Shape the dough into a ball and lightly coat it with olive oil. Place the dough in the prepared bowl, cover with plastic wrap, and let rise at room temperature for 1 to 1½ hours, until doubled in volume.

Remove the dough from the bowl and shape it into a smooth ball. The dough is ready to use immediately.

If not using the dough the same day, tightly wrap the ball in plastic wrap and refrigerate for up to 3 days. The dough can also be frozen in a freezer bag for up to 1 month.

Brunch Pizza with Pancetta, Pesto, and Eggs

Eggs on pizza. It's one of my favorite combinations because I love my eggs sunny-side up, and I love when the yolks spill over and create their own sauce. Even though this recipe has a tiny ingredient list, it is surprisingly big on flavor, thanks to the salty pancetta, fragrant pesto, and rich, runny yolks. Make the dough the night before so you'll be ready to go the next morning!

1 pound (454 g) Homemade Pizza Dough (page 90) or store-bought pizza dough

8 ounces (225 g) pancetta, cut into ¼-inch (0.6 cm) dice, or smaller

Olive oil cooking spray, for misting

½ cup (130 g) Homemade Basil-Walnut Pesto (page 90) or store-bought pesto

2 cups (230 g) shredded Colby Jack cheese

4 large eggs

—
Makes 4 servings

Bring the chilled pizza dough to room temperature for at least 30 minutes.

Prepare a hot two-zone fire in a charcoal grill (see page 10) with a grill grate over the coals.

Meanwhile, heat a medium skillet on the stovetop over medium-high heat. Add the pancetta. Cook for about 5 minutes, until brown and crispy. Set aside until ready to use.

Divide the dough in half and shape it into 2 smooth balls. Working with the first dough ball, flatten it into a disk and roll into an 8-inch (20 cm) round. Prick the dough all over with a fork and lightly mist the surface with cooking spray.

Place the dough, oiled-side down, on the grate over direct heat. Grill for about 2 minutes, until the bottom is lightly browned and the crust is barely cooked on top. Mist the top of the crust with cooking spray and turn it over.

Working quickly, spread half the pesto on the crust (all the way to the edges), followed by half each of the cheese and pancetta. Crack 2 eggs onto the pizza. (If the crust seems to be burning before you can load up all the toppings, slide it to the cooler side of the grill while you finish.)

Move the pizza over indirect heat and close the grill lid. Continue grilling until the egg whites are set but the yolks are still slightly runny, 5 to 7 minutes.

Repeat the process to make the second pizza.

Thai Chicken Pizza with Sweet Chili Sauce

When it comes to pizza, I like to experiment with non-tomato-based sauces or no sauce at all (like the Peach and Prosciutto Planked Pizza, page 91). Here, I go for a Thai-inspired flavor base with sweet chili sauce, which brings out the sweetness of the bell pepper and carrot even more. To save a little time, use leftover grilled chicken or store-bought rotisserie chicken.

1 pound (454 g) Homemade Pizza Dough (page 90) or store-bought pizza dough

1 bell pepper, any color, halved and cored

Olive oil cooking spray, for misting

½ cup (140 g) sweet chili sauce

2 cups (230 g) shredded mozzarella cheese, plus more as desired

1 cup (140 g) cooked diced chicken

½ cup (55 g) grated carrot

¼ cup (25 g) thinly sliced scallion, white and green parts

Chopped fresh cilantro, for garnishing

—

Makes 4 servings

Bring the chilled pizza dough to room temperature for at least 30 minutes.

Prepare a hot two-zone fire in a charcoal grill (see page 10) with a grill grate over the coals.

Lightly spray the bell pepper with cooking spray and place it on the grate over direct heat. Grill for 6 to 8 minutes, turning occasionally, until tender and lightly charred. Transfer to a cutting board and cut into thin strips.

Divide the dough in half and shape it into 2 smooth balls. Working with the first dough ball, flatten it into a disk and roll into an 8-inch (20 cm) round. Prick the dough all over with a fork and lightly mist the surface with cooking spray.

Place the dough, oiled-side down, on the grate over direct heat. Grill for about 2 minutes, until the bottom is lightly browned and the crust is barely cooked on top. Mist the top of the crust with cooking spray and turn it over.

Working quickly, spread half the sweet chili sauce on the crust (all the way to the edges), followed by half each of the mozzarella, chicken, carrot, scallion, and bell pepper. Sprinkle a little more mozzarella on top, if desired. (If the crust seems to be burning before you can load up all the toppings, slide it over to the cooler side of the grill while you finish.)

Move the pizza over indirect heat and close the grill lid. Continue grilling for 3 to 5 minutes, until the toppings are warm and the mozzarella is melted.

Repeat the process to make the second pizza.

Grilled Halloumi, Sweet Corn, and Tomato Salad with Basil Vinaigrette

How about a grilled cheese salad to go with all those grilled meats this summer? (Though this is not the grilled cheese you're probably thinking of!) Halloumi is a semi-hard white cheese hailing from the island of Cyprus. It has a high melting point, so it turns wonderfully creamy—not gooey—on the grill. Halloumi is comparable to a thick feta or mozzarella in texture, and while it has a salty snap right out of the package, the flavor mellows on the grill into a pleasantly savory bite. With peak-of-season ingredients like sweet corn, tomatoes, and fresh basil vinaigrette rounding out this refreshing salad, you'll find yourself bringing it to every potluck.

FOR THE VINAIGRETTE

½ cup (120 ml) olive oil

2 cups (70 g) packed fresh basil

½ shallot, coarsely chopped

1 garlic clove, coarsely chopped

2 tablespoons (30 ml) white wine vinegar

1 teaspoon kosher salt

FOR THE SALAD

8 ounces (225 g) halloumi, cut into ¼-inch (0.6 cm) slices

4 ears sweet corn, shucked

Olive oil cooking spray, for preparing the corn and cheese

1 pint (300 g) cherry tomatoes, halved

4 cups (284 g) mixed baby greens

—
Makes 4 servings

Prepare a medium-hot single-level fire in a charcoal grill (see page 10) with a grill grate over the coals.

TO MAKE THE VINAIGRETTE: In a blender, combine all the vinaigrette ingredients. Purée until smooth. Set aside until ready to use.

TO MAKE THE SALAD: Lightly spray the halloumi and corn with cooking spray. Place the halloumi on the grate. Grill for about 2 minutes per side, until charred. Arrange the corn on the grate and close the lid. Grill the corn for about 15 minutes, turning occasionally, until charred all over.

Transfer the corn and halloumi to a cutting board. Cut the kernels off the corn and slice the halloumi into small strips. Place the kernels, halloumi, tomatoes, and baby greens in a large bowl and toss to combine.

Serve the salad with a generous drizzle of vinaigrette.

HOT TIP

To keep hot kernels and juices from flying everywhere, place a small cutting board in the center of a half sheet pan. Hold the ear of corn upright and slice off the kernels with a knife. The rimmed sides of the sheet pan will contain the kernels and make it easier to collect and dump them into a bowl.

Loaded Nachos on the Grill

If there's a game on and you need something fast and easy to feed the hungry fans, these grilled nachos—loaded to the hilt with an array of awesomeness—are just the thing to tame a crowd. I actually had to hold back a little when developing this recipe because I could no longer see the chips . . . but that doesn't mean you can't add more toppings to yours! Try it with cooked ground beef, grilled shrimp, sliced fresh radishes, refried beans, shredded lettuce, guacamole, or pico de gallo for variation.

½ cup (68 g) Pickled Jalapeños (page 98)

1 cup (149 g) grape tomatoes

2 ears corn, shucked

Olive oil cooking spray, for misting

1 (12-ounce, or 340 g) bag tortilla chips

2 cups (225 g) shredded sharp Cheddar cheese

2 cups (225 g) shredded pepper Jack cheese

1 (15-ounce, or 425 g) can black beans, rinsed and drained

1 avocado, pitted and cut into small dice

3 scallions, white and green parts, thinly sliced

½ cup (8 g) chopped fresh cilantro

Sour cream, for garnishing

—
Makes 4 servings

At least one day before you plan to make the nachos, make the pickled jalapeños (page 98).

Prepare a medium-hot single-level fire in a charcoal grill (see page 10) with a grill grate over the coals.

Thread the tomatoes onto skewers. Lightly mist the tomatoes and corn with cooking spray, place them on the grate, and close the grill lid. Grill until the tomatoes are softened and slightly blistered, about 5 minutes, and the corn is charred all over and tender, about 15 minutes, turning occasionally. Transfer to a cutting board. Remove the tomatoes from the skewers and cut the kernels off the corn.

Assemble the nachos on a half sheet pan. Start by spreading the tortilla chips evenly across the pan. Follow by sprinkling half each of the Cheddar, pepper Jack, tomatoes, corn, beans, avocado, pickled jalapeños, and scallions over the chips. Repeat the layers again with the remaining toppings.

Place the sheet pan on the grate and close the grill lid. Grill for about 5 minutes, until the cheeses are melted.

Scatter the cilantro over the nachos and dot with sour cream before serving.

HOT TIP

I like to use the most battered and blackened sheet pan from my kitchen on the grill so I don't have to worry about ruining it aesthetically, but you may wish to wrap your sheet pan in heavy-duty aluminum foil. It also helps make cleanup quicker!

Pickled Jalapeños

Pickled jalapeños often find their way into many other recipes besides nachos—from eggs and toast at breakfast to steak and baked potatoes at dinner. They can be as mild or as hot as you like, so don't be afraid to try a jar!

½ cup (120 ml) distilled white vinegar

½ cup (120 ml) water

2 tablespoons (25 g) sugar

1 tablespoon (18 g) kosher salt

1 garlic clove, thinly sliced

½ teaspoon dried oregano

1½ cups (135 g) sliced jalapeño peppers

—
Makes 1½ cups (135 g)

In a small saucepan over medium-high heat, combine the vinegar, water, sugar, salt, garlic, and oregano. Bring the brine to a simmer and stir until the sugar and salt dissolve. Remove from the heat.

Pack a pint-size (480 ml) jar with the jalapeños. Pour in the brine to fill the jar. Using a spoon, tamp down on the jalapeños to submerge them in the brine. Gently run a knife around the inside edge of the jar to release any trapped air bubbles. Seal the jar with a lid and refrigerate overnight to allow the flavors to develop. The pickled jalapeños will keep, refrigerated, for up to 3 months.

HOT TIP

If you want to cut down on heat, use 3 tablespoons (37.5 g) of sugar in the brine for sweeter pickles.

Grilled Corn with Sweet Chili–Soy Glaze

In my opinion, no summer barbecue is complete without a pile of piping-hot fresh corn right off the grill. I like mine shucked before they hit the grate; the fire concentrates the sugars in the kernels, making them sweeter, at the same time adding a smoky char quintessential to grilling. Here, I intensify those natural flavors with an Asian-inspired glaze that's sweet, savory, and flecked with a little heat.

2 tablespoons (30 ml)
soy sauce

2 tablespoons (40 g) sweet
chili sauce

6 ears corn, shucked

Olive oil cooking spray,
for misting

Butter, for serving (optional)

—

Makes 6 servings

Prepare a medium-hot single-level fire in a charcoal grill (see page 10) with a grill grate over the coals.

In a small bowl, stir together the soy sauce and sweet chili sauce. Set aside until needed.

Mist the corn with cooking spray, arrange the ears on the grate, and close the grill lid. Grill for 5 to 10 minutes, turning occasionally, until the corn begins to char. Brush the glaze on the corn and continue grilling, with the lid closed, until the kernels are tender and charred all over, about 10 minutes, turning every 3 minutes and brushing with more glaze.

Serve with another slather of glaze on the corn and a swipe of butter, if desired.

Grilled Lobster Tails with Lemony Herb Butter

Grilled lobster tail sounds like an expensive and extravagant feast to pull off, but therein lies the benefit of grilling at home: you can have a luxe meal for much less than you'd spend eating out. And in my family, we almost always prefer going **outside** for our food, rather than just going **out**, because of this! The flavor you get from the luscious lemon-herb compound butter rivals (and perhaps surpasses) one you'd be served in a restaurant.

FOR THE HERB BUTTER

8 tablespoons (1 stick, or 112 g) butter, at room temperature

¼ cup (weight varies) minced fresh herbs

2 tablespoons (20 g) minced garlic

1 teaspoon lemon zest

1 teaspoon fresh lemon juice

FOR THE LOBSTERS

4 (8-ounce, or 225 g) lobster tails

Olive oil cooking spray, for misting

Kosher salt

Ground black pepper

Lemon wedges, for serving

—
Makes 4 servings

Prepare a medium single-level fire in a charcoal grill (see page 10) with a grill grate over the coals.

TO MAKE THE HERB BUTTER: In a small bowl, using a fork, mash and stir the butter, herbs, garlic, lemon zest, and lemon juice until well combined. Set aside until needed.

To butterfly the lobster tails:

1. Place each lobster tail, shell-side up, on a cutting board. Using heavy-duty kitchen shears, line up the bottom blade right under the shell and cut lengthwise down the center, stopping at the base of the tail. (The tail fin should remain intact.)

2. With a knife, cut along the same line to split the meat, stopping just before you slice all the way through to the bottom.

3. Turn the lobster tail over and snip the horizontal spines down the middle of the tail with your shears. If there are little fin-like legs (swimmerets) attached, snip those off and discard them.

4. Turn the lobster tail over again and pry it open like a book to separate and expose the meat.

Mist the meat with cooking spray and season with salt and pepper. Arrange the lobster tails, meat-side down, on the grate and close the grill lid. Grill for 5 to 7 minutes, until lightly charred.

Flip the lobsters onto their shells and brush the flesh generously with the compound butter, using about 2 tablespoons (28 g) per lobster. Close the grill lid and grill for about 5 minutes, until the flesh is opaque and firm to the touch and an instant-read thermometer inserted into the lobster registers 135°F (57°C). Serve the lobster tails with lemon wedges on the side.

Empty Beer Can Chicken

So, why do I call this **empty** beer can chicken? Contrary to popular belief, stuffing a can full of beer up a chicken's butt is just a waste of good beer. Real flavor comes from the smoky aroma inside a grill and the seasoning you use on the outside of the chicken—not from any fancy craft beer you sacrifice to the grill. Juicy meat comes from proper roasting technique, not from beer magically bubbling out of a can and steaming the chicken.

What beer can chicken does get right, however, is utilizing a method called vertical roasting. Vertical roasting helps the meat heat more evenly because the legs (being closer to the coals) cook faster than the breasts, so the whole bird can be taken off the grill without being over- or undercooked. It also results in crisp, crackly skin, as the upright orientation drains fat well.

So save that beer (or whatever cold beverage you like to imbibe) for drinking, and, once you're done with it, repurpose it as a cheap and efficient roasting stand on the grill.

1 (12-ounce, or 360 ml) can of your favorite beverage

FOR THE SPICE RUB

3 tablespoons (45 g) packed light brown sugar

2 tablespoons (36 g) kosher salt

1 tablespoon (8 g) smoked paprika

1 tablespoon (8 g) sweet paprika

1 tablespoon (5 g) cayenne pepper

FOR THE CHICKEN

1 (4-pound, or 1.8 kg) whole chicken, giblets removed

—
Makes 4 servings

Prepare a medium three-zone fire in a charcoal grill (see page 10) with a drip pan placed between the coals and a grill grate over the coals.

While you work, enjoy a can of your favorite beverage until empty and set aside.

TO MAKE THE SPICE RUB: In a small bowl, stir together all the rub ingredients. Set aside until ready to use. The spice rub can be stored in an airtight container in a cool, dark, dry place for up to 6 months (after which it starts to lose potency).

TO MAKE THE CHICKEN: Pat the chicken dry with paper towels. Liberally season the chicken all over with the spice rub (store any unused spice rub for future use).

Insert the empty can into the chicken's cavity and tuck the wings close to the body. Place the chicken on the grate over indirect heat, above the drip pan. Balance the chicken carefully on the can so the can and the two legs act as a tripod to keep it stable and upright. Close the grill lid.

Roast the chicken for 45 to 60 minutes (depending on the heat of your grill), until the skin is crisp and brown and an instant-read thermometer inserted into the chicken registers

160°F (71°C) in the breast (closest to the ribs without touching bone). If needed, add a few unlit pieces of charcoal about 20 minutes into roasting to maintain consistent heat.

Transfer the chicken to a cutting board and let rest for 10 minutes before carving. Serve the chicken with the pan drippings.

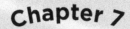

Chapter 7

Feasting ...
with Smoke

Rooted in Native American history, plank grilling
originated from Pacific Northwest tribes cooking their
salmon on cedar slabs over an open flame. While salmon
is still commonly associated with this method, modern-
day planking gives us many more options for the grill—
from fruits and vegetables to pizza and meatloaf.

What makes it so special is that a plank of wood is more
than just a pretty platter. Planks infuse the food with a
sweet, smoky aroma, adding depth to even the blandest
ingredients. Flavorful juices don't drip off into the fire,
so food stays rich and succulent. Small or delicate foods
won't fall apart or slip through the grate. And, for the
newly initiated, planks are also forgiving; you can leave
(forget?) the food for a few extra minutes and it will still
be waiting for you.

Choosing a Plank

When choosing a plank for your grill, you have to consider two things: size and type of wood.

Most grilling planks are ⅜ to ½ inch (0.9 to 1 cm) thick and measure 12 x 7 inches (30 x 18 cm). This is the minimum size you'll need for all the planking recipes in this book. Some grilling planks also come in squares, ovals, and individual serving sizes, so you can match plank to food for both practicality and presentation.

The most common plank wood is Western red cedar. If you're only going to get one type of wood, you can't go wrong with cedar; if you're open to experimentation, stock a variety of grilling planks in your outdoor kitchen and discover how each type of wood infuses your food with its own distinct aroma.

Western red cedar has a strong, spicy, and smoky sweet flavor that works well with fish, seafood, vegetables, fruits, and soft cheeses.

Hickory has a heavy, intense flavor that pairs perfectly with beef, lamb, wild game, and bacon.

Oak falls in the middle of the spectrum with its bold, but not overpowering, flavor. It complements a wide range of foods, including beef, chicken, pork, and fish.

Cherry is a fruity, smoky wood whose sweetness pairs well with chicken, turkey, lamb, and duck.

Maple is a subtly sweet wood with a balanced flavor, so it goes well with many foods, such as pork, chicken, turkey, vegetables, fruits, and cheeses.

Alder has a mild, earthy, and slightly nutty flavor that complements white fish, seafood, vegetables, and fruits.

Preparing the Plank for Grilling

Step 1: Soaking: Start by soaking the plank in water for at least 1 hour (or overnight). If you're feeling creative, you can soak the plank in beer, white wine, apple juice, or other liquids for a little extra flavor.

This important step not only keeps the plank from catching fire and over-charring, but it also helps the plank last longer, so you can reuse it. I like to soak my planks in a baking dish with a heavy pot to weight them down, and I usually flip them halfway through to ensure they're thoroughly soaked.

HOT TIP

If you often forget to soak planks before you want to grill, soak them ahead of time. Wrap the soaked planks in plastic bags and store them in the freezer. The frozen planks can be preheated on the grill without thawing (just allow a few extra minutes for the wood to start smoking).

Step 2: Preheating: Preheating the plank serves two purposes: to control warping (as most woods, with the exception of cedar, tend to warp when placed over heat) and impart a deeper wood flavor to the food.

Begin by firing up your charcoal grill. Arrange the coals into a two-zone fire (see page 10) with a grill grate over the coals. Place the soaked plank on the grate over direct heat and close the grill lid. Let it preheat for about 5 minutes. When you see wisps of light gray smoke emanating from the grill, open the lid and check the plank. If it hasn't bowed, you can start grilling. If it's warped, using tongs, flip the plank over and close the lid again. Let it heat for a couple more minutes until it flattens out.

Grilling with the Plank

Once the plank is preheated, using tongs, flip it over and move it over indirect heat. Place your food on the scorched side of the plank and close the grill lid. Grill as directed in the recipe instructions. Adjust the dampers as needed to maintain a consistent temperature and light gray smoke (see page 89 for more on using the grill's dampers).

To remove the plank from the grill, firmly grip the edge closest to you with tongs and slide the plank onto a sheet pan. Remember, the plank will be very hot, as will the bottom of the sheet pan when you carry it to the table. The food can be served on the plank or plated individually for guests.

Cleaning and Storing the Plank

As you do with dishes, soak the plank in water to loosen any food remnants. Scrub it with soap and water and rinse well to remove any soap residue. Let the plank air-dry completely to prevent molding before storing.

A used plank can be cleaned, dried, soaked, and reused two to four times before it becomes too blackened. Alternate the sides you preheat each time so the wood chars more evenly, prolonging the plank's usability. Try to reuse the same plank to grill the same types of food, particularly fish and seafood. Once the plank has reached the end of its life, you can break it apart with a hammer and use it as smoking wood.

Planked Pears with Gorgonzola and Honey

If I'm already making dinner on the grill, I usually make dessert on the grill, too. Grilled fruit (or in this case, grill-roasted fruit) takes the agony out of deciding what to serve when the last of the plates have been scraped off and your guests are settling into a long night of storytelling.

It's simple: a platter of sweet, caramelized pears, sharpened with creamy Gorgonzola, and washed down with your favorite digestif.

1 tablespoon (14 g) butter, at room temperature

1 tablespoon (20 g) honey

2 pears, halved lengthwise and cored (see note)

¼ cup (30 g) crumbled Gorgonzola cheese

—
Makes 4 servings

Soak a cedar plank in water for at least 1 hour before you plan to grill.

Prepare a medium-hot two-zone fire in a charcoal grill (see page 10) with a grill grate over the coals.

In a small bowl, stir together the butter and honey until well blended. Brush the cut sides of the pears generously with the butter mixture and sprinkle the Gorgonzola on top.

Preheat the plank until it starts to smoke (see page 106). Turn the plank over and move it to indirect heat. Arrange the pears on the plank and close the grill lid. Roast for about 25 minutes, until the pears are tender and scorched around the edges.

Cedar-Planked Tomatoes Stuffed with Mushrooms and Gruyère

By their nature, stuffed tomatoes aren't grand—they're comfort food. They're made at home, served with a simple scoop of rice, and you'll rarely find them on a menu at your local French or Vietnamese restaurant.

Tomates farcies, as they're called in French, were a staple of my childhood. Though my family's version leans traditional Vietnamese, I've always liked to tinker with the ingredients to make peak-season tomatoes really shine. This is one of my favorite versions and a good use for tomatoes "on the vine" at the market, as the green stems make lovely little handles on the "hats" for serving.

8 ripe but firm tomatoes (about 4 ounces, or 115 g each, or 2 pounds, or 908 g total), preferably with stems attached

½ cup (25 g) fine fresh bread crumbs, from day-old bread

½ cup (60 g) grated Gruyère cheese, plus more for sprinkling

½ cup (35 g) finely chopped cremini mushrooms

½ cup (80 g) minced shallot

2 tablespoons (8 g) minced fresh parsley

2 tablespoons (5 g) minced fresh basil

2 garlic cloves, minced

1 teaspoon minced fresh thyme

½ teaspoon kosher salt

¼ teaspoon ground black pepper

2 tablespoons (30 ml) olive oil, plus more for drizzling

—
Makes 4 servings

Soak a cedar plank in water for at least 1 hour before you plan to grill.

Prepare a medium-hot two-zone fire in a charcoal grill (see page 10) with a grill grate over the coals.

Using a paring knife, cut off the top ½ inch (1 cm) from each tomato, reserving the top, and cut out the core. Using a spoon, scoop out the innards, leaving a ½-inch (1 cm)-thick shell. Save the juices, seeds, and flesh to make the marinara sauce on page 112, or discard. Arrange the tomatoes (with their accompanying tops) on a sheet pan and set aside.

In a medium bowl, stir together the bread crumbs, Gruyère, mushrooms, shallot, parsley, basil, garlic, thyme, salt, pepper, and olive oil. Stuff each tomato with 3 to 4 tablespoons (18 to 24 g) of the bread crumb mixture and top with a sprinkle of Gruyère. Place the tops back on the tomatoes, like little hats, and drizzle with olive oil.

Preheat the plank until it starts to smoke (see page 106). Turn the plank over and move it to indirect heat. Arrange the tomatoes on the plank and close the grill lid. Grill for about 30 minutes, until the tomatoes are soft, the filling is golden brown, and the cheese is melted.

Planked Meatballs with Marinara Sauce

Part of being a good and efficient cook is knowing where to focus your efforts and where to take shortcuts—and this is especially true for these planked meatballs with marinara sauce. While I always prefer homemade meatballs, my butcher sells a fine selection of meatballs I'm happy to use on nights when I just want to get dinner done. The woodsy flavor from the plank makes any meatball that much better, and the homemade marinara (which comes together quickly and easily) beats any from a jar.

I like these meatballs on a bed of spaghetti with more sauce on top, but you can also layer them between slider buns with fresh basil, tuck them inside hoagie rolls with melted provolone, or spear them with toothpicks to serve as an appetizer.

FOR THE MARINARA SAUCE

2 tablespoons (30 ml) olive oil

1 shallot, minced

2 garlic cloves, minced

1 (28-ounce, or 790 g) can whole peeled tomatoes, undrained

1 tablespoon (4 g) minced fresh oregano

Pinch red pepper flakes

Kosher salt

FOR THE MEATBALLS

12 (about 1 pound, or 454 g) Italian-style meatballs

Kosher salt

Ground black pepper

Grated Parmesan cheese, for sprinkling

Cooked spaghetti, for serving (optional)

—

Makes 4 servings

Soak an oak plank in water for at least 1 hour before you plan to grill.

Prepare a medium-hot two-zone fire in a charcoal grill (see page 10) with a grill grate over the coals.

TO MAKE THE MARINARA SAUCE: On the stovetop, heat a medium skillet over medium-high heat. Add the olive oil and shallot. Cook for 1 to 2 minutes, until the shallot is translucent. Stir in the garlic, tomatoes, oregano, and red pepper flakes and bring the sauce to a rapid simmer. Reduce the heat and keep the sauce at a slow, steady simmer, stirring occasionally and mashing the tomatoes with the back of a spoon as they break down. Cook for at least 30 minutes until ready to use. The longer the sauce simmers, the thicker and richer it becomes. Taste the sauce and add salt if needed. (If you prefer a smoother sauce, blend it before using.)

TO MAKE THE MEATBALLS: Season the meatballs with salt and pepper.

Preheat the plank until it starts to smoke (see page 106). Turn the plank over and move it to indirect heat. Arrange the meatballs on the plank and close the grill lid. Grill for about 10 minutes, until the meatballs are browned all over.

Spoon about 1 tablespoon (15 g) of marinara sauce over each meatball. (Reserve unused marinara for future use or to coat spaghetti for a full meal.) Close the grill lid and grill for about 5 minutes.

Sprinkle Parmesan over the meatballs and close the grill lid. Grill for 5 minutes more, until the cheese melts. An instant-read thermometer inserted into the center of the meatball should register 160°F (71°C). Serve with more Parmesan sprinkled on top and cooked spaghetti, if desired.

HOT TIP

If you want to try your hand at homemade meatballs, follow my recipe for Bacon-Wrapped Meatloaf on a Plank (page 118)—omitting the bacon—and shape the mixture into 1½-inch (3.5 cm) balls. Cook as instructed above.

Cedar-Planked Hot Ham and Brie Melts

Ham and Brie on a plank is one of my favorite twists on the traditional grilled cheese. The cedar plank infuses the sandwiches with a subtle aroma that seems to enhance the earthiness of soft-ripened Brie. I like to finish them directly on the grill for a few minutes to add a little crispness and char to the bread.

8 slices country bread

Mayonnaise, for spreading

Dijon mustard, for spreading

8 to 12 ounces (225 to 340 g) deli ham, thinly sliced

1 (8-ounce, or 225 g) wheel Brie cheese, cut into ¼-inch (0.6 cm) slices (see note)

Hot Pepper Jelly (page 116) or store-bought hot pepper jelly, for spreading

—
Makes 4 servings

Soak a cedar plank in water for at least 1 hour before you plan to grill.

Prepare a medium-hot two-zone fire in a charcoal grill (see page 10) with a grill grate over the coals.

On 4 bread slices, spread a thin coat of mayonnaise on one side. Flip the bread and spread a thin coat of Dijon on the other side. Layer a few slices each of the ham and cheese on top.

On the remaining 4 bread slices, slather the jelly. Place them, jelly-side down, on the sandwich. Spread a thin coat of mayonnaise on top.

Preheat the plank until it starts to smoke (see page 106). Turn the plank over and move it over indirect heat. Arrange the sandwiches on the plank and close the grill lid. Grill for 10 to 12 minutes, until the cheese is melted and the bread is toasted. Remove the sandwiches from the plank and move them over to the direct heat side. Grill the sandwiches on the grate, uncovered, for about 1 minute per side, until good grill marks form.

Hot Pepper Jelly

The sweet heat of this pepper jelly pairs beautifully with the creamy Brie and tangy mustard in my Cedar-Planked Hot Ham and Brie Melts (page 114), but you'll also love this on biscuits and crostini, glazed onto chicken or pork, or layered on other soft cheeses such as Camembert.

2 cups (300 g) finely chopped bell peppers, any color or a mix

½ cup (120 ml) apple cider vinegar

1 teaspoon red pepper flakes

3 tablespoons (36 g) Sure-Jell Less or No Sugar Needed Premium Fruit Pectin

1 teaspoon butter

1½ cups (300 g) sugar

—

Makes 3 (8-ounce, or 225 g) jars

HOT TIP

Make sure your red pepper flakes are fresh for the best flavor! You can also use any combination of peppers in this recipe to make the jelly as hot or mild as you prefer. In place of red pepper flakes, try a fresh hot chile, such as serrano or habanero (if you like a little kick), or a jalapeño for a tamer flavor.

To prepare your jars and lids, place them in a large saucepan and cover with at least 1 inch (2.5 cm) of water. Heat them on the stovetop over medium heat and keep them warm while you make the jelly. (Alternatively, wash them in the dishwasher right before you begin so they'll remain warm after the heated drying cycle.)

In a wide heavy-bottomed saucepan over medium-high heat, combine the bell peppers, vinegar, and red pepper flakes. Stir in the pectin and butter. Bring the mixture to a full rolling boil (a vigorous boil that doesn't stop bubbling when stirred), stirring constantly. Stir in the sugar. Return the mixture to a full rolling boil and boil for 1 minute, stirring constantly. Remove the saucepan from the heat.

Drain the jars and place them on a clean kitchen towel. Ladle the hot jelly into the warm jars, filling to within ½ inch (1 cm) of the rims. Stir the jelly to redistribute the peppers (they have a tendency to float), and seal the jars with lids. Let them come to room temperature before refrigerating. The jelly should set overnight or within 24 hours. The jelly will keep, refrigerated, for up to 3 weeks.

Planked Halibut with Orange-Miso Glaze

Thick and meaty, firm yet flaky, halibut has a heartier texture and flavor than most other white fish on the market. It's a bit more forgiving because it won't overcook as easily as thinner fillets, and it can handle a little more time on the grill, which means more time to infuse all that wonderfully smoky flavor. For all these reasons, I like to pair halibut with a cedar plank and a zippy orange-miso sauce flecked with ginger. As it cooks on the grill, the sauce turns into a shimmering glaze that stands up perfectly to the hefty fillet.

2 tablespoons (40 g) orange marmalade

2 tablespoons (34 g) white or yellow miso

1 teaspoon sesame oil

1 teaspoon soy sauce

1 teaspoon mirin

1 teaspoon grated peeled fresh ginger

4 (8-ounce, or 225 g) halibut fillets

Toasted sesame seeds, for garnishing

Finely chopped scallions, white and green parts, for garnishing

—

Makes 4 servings

Soak a cedar plank in water for at least 1 hour before you plan to grill.

Prepare a medium-hot two-zone fire in a charcoal grill (see page 10) with a grill grate over the coals.

In a small bowl, whisk the marmalade, miso, sesame oil, soy sauce, mirin, and ginger until combined.

Thoroughly pat the halibut dry with paper towels and generously brush the fillets with the glaze.

Preheat the plank until it starts to smoke (see page 106). Turn the plank over and move it over indirect heat. Arrange the halibut on the plank and close the grill lid. Grill for 15 to 20 minutes, until an instant-read thermometer inserted into the thickest part of the flesh reaches 130°F to 135°F (54°C to 57°C). (Depending on the thickness of your fillets, cooking time may vary by a few minutes.)

Garnish with sesame seeds and scallions before serving.

Bacon-Wrapped Meatloaf on a Plank

Meatloaf on the grill. It's every bit as amazing as you might imagine. At first thought, it doesn't sound like it could work from a logistical standpoint. But enter a grilling plank and—suddenly—you can use the fragrant smoke of the wood to your advantage.

There are endless variations on the classic Americana recipe, but these are a few of my favorite tricks for achieving a gorgeous, succulent, and tender meatloaf: sauté the vegetables first to enhance flavor and moisture; use a blend of freshly ground chuck and Italian sausage for extra richness; mix in rolled oats to retain all those delicious juices; and add bacon because . . . well, bacon. Your favorite barbecue sauce just sends it over the top!

2 tablespoons (28 g) butter

⅓ cup (53 g) minced onion

⅓ cup (37 g) minced carrot

⅓ cup (50 g) minced bell pepper, any color

2 garlic cloves, minced

6 thin bacon slices

2 large eggs, beaten

1 tablespoon (15 ml) Worcestershire sauce

1 tablespoon (6 g) ground black pepper

2 teaspoons kosher salt

1 teaspoon smoked paprika

½ cup (78 g) old-fashioned rolled oats

½ cup (125 g) of your favorite barbecue sauce, plus more for glazing

1 pound (454 g) ground chuck

1 pound (454 g) bulk mild Italian sausage

—

Makes 6 servings

Soak an oak or cedar plank in water for at least 1 hour before you plan to grill.

Prepare a medium-hot two-zone fire in a charcoal grill (see page 10) or, preferably if your grill is large enough, a three-zone fire (see page 10) with a grill grate over the coals.

On the stovetop, in a medium skillet over medium-high heat, melt the butter. Add the onion, carrot, and bell pepper. Stir to combine. Cook for 6 to 8 minutes, until the onion is translucent and the carrot has softened. Stir in the garlic. Cook for about 1 minute, until very fragrant. Remove from the heat and set aside.

Line a loaf pan with parchment paper. Drape the bacon in a crisscross pattern across the loaf pan and leave the ends hanging over the edge.

In a large bowl, combine the eggs, Worcestershire, pepper, salt, paprika, oats, barbecue sauce, and cooked vegetables. Add the ground chuck and Italian sausage. Work the ingredients together by hand until just combined (avoid overmixing).

Soak an oak or cedar plank in water for at least 1 hour before you plan to grill.

Prepare a medium-hot two-zone fire in a charcoal grill (see page 10) or, preferably if your grill is large enough, a three-zone fire (see page 10) with a grill grate over the coals.

On the stovetop, in a medium skillet over medium-high heat, melt the butter. Add the onion, carrot, and bell pepper. Stir to combine.

Cook for 6 to 8 minutes, until the onion is translucent and the carrot has softened. Stir in the garlic. Cook for about 1 minute, until very fragrant. Remove from the heat and set aside.

Line a loaf pan with parchment paper. Drape the bacon in a crisscross pattern across the loaf pan and leave the ends hanging over the edge.

In a large bowl, combine the eggs, Worcestershire, pepper, salt, paprika, oats, barbecue sauce, and cooked vegetables. Add the ground chuck and Italian sausage. Work the ingredients together by hand until just combined (avoid overmixing).

(At this stage, you can cook a spoonful of the mixture in a skillet to taste and adjust any seasonings, if desired. This is an optional step but helpful if you want to know how your barbecue sauce works with the recipe.)

Pat the meatloaf mixture into your prepared loaf pan and fold the bacon ends over the meatloaf.

Preheat the plank until it starts to smoke (see page 106). Put on a pair of heatproof gloves, turn the plank over, and place the toasted side on top of your loaf pan. Then, holding onto the plank and the pan so they're tight against each other, turn both over and place them on the indirect heat side of the grill. Carefully slide the pan off the meatloaf (using the parchment to help you, if necessary) and discard the parchment. Close the grill lid. Grill for about 30 minutes, until the bacon is crisp and brown on the edges and the meatloaf has formed a crust.

Brush the top of the meatloaf with more barbecue sauce and close the grill lid. Continue grilling for 20 to 30 minutes more, until an instant-read thermometer inserted into the center of the meatloaf reaches 155°F (68°C). (If you have a two-zone fire, rotate the plank 180 degrees at this halfway point for even cooking.)

Let the meatloaf rest for 10 minutes before slicing and serving.

HOT TIP

If you don't have a loaf pan, spoon the meatloaf mixture onto the preheated plank and pat it into a 9 x 5-inch (23 x 13 cm) loaf-shaped mound. Cut the bacon strips in half, drape them over the meatloaf, and grill, following the instructions as listed.

Peach and Prosciutto Planked Pizza

Using an aromatic wood plank is a worthwhile alternative to grilling on a pizza stone or directly on the grate. It infuses the crust with a light, smoky flavor, keeps the dough from burning underneath, and makes a great presentation on the table. I like to make this vibrant pizza—full of sweet, ripe peaches, fragrant basil, and wisps of salty prosciutto—when I'm looking to do something a little different from my usual veggie garden and pepperoni pie.

1 pound (454 g) Homemade Pizza Dough (page 90) or store-bought pizza dough

1 teaspoon olive oil

1 teaspoon balsamic vinegar

Kosher salt

Ground black pepper

1 to 1½ peaches, pitted, halved, and cut into ½-inch (1 cm) wedges

Olive oil cooking spray, for misting

Coarse-grind cornmeal, for dusting

2 cups (230 g) shredded mozzarella cheese

6 thin slices prosciutto, torn into pieces

¼ red onion, thinly sliced

½ cup (75 g) crumbled goat cheese

Handful thinly sliced fresh basil

—
Makes 4 servings

HOT TIP

To form a rectangular pizza that will fit your plank, shape the dough into a cylinder and roll it out on a smooth surface. Drape the dough over a clean spare plank. With your fingers, shape or roll up the edges as needed to fit perfectly on the plank. The dough can then be pricked all over with a fork, misted with cooking spray, and carefully flipped over on top of your preheated plank.

Soak two maple or alder planks in water for at least 1 hour before you plan to grill.

Bring the chilled pizza dough to room temperature for at least 30 minutes.

Prepare a medium-hot two-zone fire in a charcoal grill (see page 10) with a grill grate over the coals.

In a small bowl, whisk the olive oil, vinegar, and a pinch each of salt and pepper until well blended. Add the peach wedges and toss to coat. Set aside until needed.

Divide the dough in half and shape each portion into a long smooth cylinder. Roll each cylinder into a rectangle about the size of your plank (see tip). Prick the dough all over with a fork and mist the surface with cooking spray.

Preheat the first plank until it starts to smoke (see page 106). Turn the plank over and move it over indirect heat. Dust the surface with a handful of cornmeal (to keep the dough from sticking). Place the first dough, oiled-side down, on the plank and mist the top with cooking spray. Close the grill lid. Grill for 5 to 7 minutes, until lightly browned and slightly crisp.

Working quickly, spread half the mozzarella on the crust (all the way to the edges), followed by half each of the prosciutto, onion, peaches, and goat cheese. Close the grill lid. Continue grilling for 5 to 7 minutes, until the cheese is golden and bubbly and the toppings are warmed through.

Garnish the pizza with basil before serving. Repeat the process with the second plank to make the second pizza.

Chapter 8

Outdoor Sweets

Sticky spoons and forks drip with sweet sustenance. In just a few seconds, they're licked clean. Crumpled napkins sit on empty plates as the coals burn out, the sky turns a deeper black, and the stars glow brighter. Conversations quiet into comfortable silence. You feel your body aligning itself with the rhythm of the earth, and in that moment, life is complete.

Campfire S'mores, 6 Ways

A camping cookbook just isn't complete without s'mores! But you don't need a recipe to tell you how to toast a marshmallow. Rather, think of these "recipes" as inspiration for your next campfire concoction when you want to jazz up the usual marshmallow, chocolate, and graham cracker stack.

STRAWBERRY S'MORES

Toasted marshmallows

Strawberries (fresh or warmed over the fire)

Dark chocolate

Graham crackers

PEANUT BUTTER AND BANANA S'MORES

Toasted marshmallows

Sliced bananas

Reese's Peanut Butter Cups

Chocolate graham crackers

CHOCOLATE CHIP COOKIE S'MORES

Toasted marshmallows

Milk chocolate

Soft-baked chocolate chip cookies

NUTELLA AND SALTED CARAMEL S'MORES

Toasted marshmallows

Nutella

Salted caramel chocolate

Graham crackers

ALMOND BUTTER AND JELLY S'MORES

Toasted marshmallows

Raspberry jelly

Almond butter

Dark chocolate with almonds

Graham crackers

NUTTY CARAMEL S'MORES

Toasted marshmallows

Crunchy peanut butter

Caramel chocolate

Chocolate graham crackers

S'mores Tips & Tricks

Everyone has an idea of the perfect s'more. Should the chocolate be melted or not? Should the marshmallow be well charred or just golden brown? While there's no right or wrong when it comes to making the classic treat, I've toasted (and burned) many a s'more in my life, so here are a few things I've learned along the way.

You don't have to toast a marshmallow on a stick.

In fact, you don't need skewers at all. Simply assemble your s'more in the center of a sheet of heavy-duty foil, wrap it up tightly, and place it on the grill grate or near the coals for a few minutes. Use tongs to retrieve your foil pack. The marshmallow won't have a golden crust, but it'll be perfectly gooey, along with the chocolate and other ingredients.

A toasted marshmallow doesn't actually melt the chocolate.

The residual heat from a hot-off-the-flame marshmallow might make the top of the chocolate glisten, but it certainly won't melt it into an oozing cascade. Instead, melt your ingredients separately. Place a square of chocolate on a graham cracker, and set it over indirect heat on the grill grate. Pull it off once the chocolate has melted sufficiently, and top with a toasted marshmallow.

It's easy to make s'mores for a crowd.

To melt several s'mores at the same time (or if you have quite the raging fire going), place a cast-iron pan on the grate and arrange your chocolate-laden graham crackers in the pan. Transfer them to plates with a spatula once melted. The pan method also helps prevent your crackers from scorching or falling through the grate. Campers will want to toast their own marshmallows, of course!

You don't need a campfire to make s'mores.

If you have a portable grill with a lid, you can make s'mores without making a fire. Stack a graham cracker, chocolate, and marshmallow on the grate, leave the whole thing under the lid for a few minutes, and the ingredients will melt beautifully.

You can let your imagination run wild.

If you've never ventured outside of graham cracker/milk chocolate/marshmallow territory, you are in for a treat.

Step up your s'more game with different kinds of crackers and cookies, like flavored graham crackers (cinnamon or chocolate), oatmeal cookies, vanilla wafers, gingersnaps, or stroopwafel. Even pound cake, brownies, Pop-Tarts, or Rice Krispies treats can serve as tasty bases!

Explore different types of chocolate, like white, dark, and extra dark chocolate, or artisanal flavors like salted caramel, chile orange, and mint chocolate.

Experiment with your favorite jams, jellies, or nut butters, as well as caramel sauce, chocolate syrup, or fresh berries.

SOME MORE HISORY

The history of the s'more is somewhat vague, but the first recipe for "Some Mores" was published in 1927 in a handbook called Tramping and Trailing with the Girl Scouts. Though the recipe was credited to a woman named Loretta Scott Crew, sources are conflicted on whether she actually invented the sticky snack or was merely the first to be formally credited for it. The original recipe instructs Girl Scouts to "Toast two marshmallows over the coals to a crisp gooey state and then put them inside a graham cracker and chocolate bar sandwich. . . . Though it tastes like 'some more,' one is really enough." As for when "some more" became "s'more," the contracted term came a decade later in various publications and has stuck ever since.

HIGH-ALTITUDE BAKING TIP

If you're making a dutch baby in camp at an elevation above 3,000 feet (900 m), a quick and dirty trick for helping the pancake puff up is to use extra-large eggs or high-protein flour in the batter, or both. The science behind this is to increase the protein sources so that coagulation can occur before the structure collapses (as a result of low air pressure). For campsites at 5,000 feet (1,500 m), try adding 1 large egg plus 1 to 2 tablespoons flour to the batter. For campsites at 8,000 feet (2,400 m) or above, try adding 2 large eggs plus 2 to 4 tablespoons flour to the batter.

Remember that elevation and humidity can vary greatly on every camping trip, so you may need to experiment with varying amounts of egg and flour before you find the perfect ratio. But no worries if your dutch baby doesn't pass the puff test—it will still be delicious.

Applelicious Dutch Baby

A dutch baby is one of those dishes that can go from breakfast to dessert and back to breakfast again. It's basically an eggy pancake—or a marriage of a pancake and a popover, if you will. Though it's typically served for breakfast, a dutch baby makes a sweetly satisfying dessert when topped with lots of luscious fresh fruit and warm brown sugar. (At home, try it with a scoop of ice cream!) It's sometimes called a German pancake, from which it was derived, and the term *Dutch* refers to the German-speaking immigrants known as the Pennsylvania Dutch.

1 cup (120 g) all-purpose flour

½ cup (106 g) packed brown sugar, divided

½ teaspoon ground cinnamon, divided

6 large eggs

1 cup (240 ml) milk

Olive oil spray

¼ cup (56 g) butter

3 medium apples, cored and cut into ¼-inch (6-mm) slices

Powdered sugar

—
Makes 6 servings

MIX IT UP

Try this recipe with pears, or half apples and half pears. If it's summertime and you want to take advantage of seasonal berries (imagine how beautiful it would be if you could forage wild blackberries near camp?), bake the dutch baby with any combination of berries and scatter a handful of fresh berries on top before serving.

AT HOME: Combine the flour, ¼ cup (103 g) of the brown sugar, and ¼ teaspoon of the cinnamon in a resealable plastic bag and store in a dry, cool place until ready to use.

IN CAMP: Prepare a mound of wood coals, hardwood lump charcoal, or charcoal briquettes (see page 8).

Meanwhile, whisk together the eggs, milk, and flour mixture in a medium bowl until well blended.

Move about a quart's worth of coals to the cooking pit and arrange them in a ring (see page 71). Lightly spray a dutch oven with oil and heat it over the coals. Melt the butter in the oven, then pour in the egg mixture. Spread the apples evenly over the surface and sprinkle with the remaining ¼ cup (103 g) sugar and the remaining ¼ teaspoon cinnamon. Cover and place 1½ rings of coals on the lid.

Bake over medium heat for 20 to 25 minutes, or until the pancake is puffed and golden all over. (Call the kids over to ooh and ahh at your creation once you take the oven off the heat, because the pancake will deflate shortly after the lid is removed.)

Dust the pancake with powdered sugar before serving.

Grilled Pears with Honey-Cinnamon Crème Fraîche

These pears are light and silky and pair nicely with a glass of rosé or white wine, which is always a good way to end the day.

2 tablespoons honey

2 teaspoons ground cinnamon

1 cup (227 g) crème fraîche

4 pears, halved and cored

—
Makes 4 servings

Prepare a grill over medium-high heat.

Meanwhile, stir the honey and cinnamon into the crème fraîche (right in the container for easy cleanup) until well combined.

Place the pears on the grill and cook for 3 to 5 minutes, turning once, until the pears are softened with good grill marks.

Serve each pear with a dollop of the sweetened crème fraîche.

Sweet Caramelized Figs and Peaches

If your sweet tooth is aching after dinner but you don't feel like making a production out of dessert, these caramelized figs and peaches will satisfy on both counts. Just a few minutes in a browned butter glaze brings out their richness without overpowering their fresh flavor. Serve them with a slice of pound cake, or spoon over yogurt for a lighter option.

2 tablespoons butter

2 tablespoons packed
brown sugar

4 medium figs, halved lengthwise

2 medium peaches, pitted and sliced

—
Makes 4 servings

In a small saucepan over medium heat, melt the butter. Add the sugar and stir until the mixture turns frothy and golden brown, about 2 minutes.

Add the figs and peaches and stir to coat. Cook until the fruits start to soften and release their juices, about 3 minutes, stirring occasionally.

Divide the fruit among serving plates, spooning the glaze over the fruits.

Whiskey-Spiked Sweet Tea

Iced tea cocktails like this one are a modern spin on mixed drinks that let both beverages shine. The whiskey here (I like to use Tennessee whiskey) adds just enough bite to counter the sweetness of the Southern-style tea. But be warned: It goes down way too easily.

7 cups (17 dL) water

1 cup (100 g) sugar

3 family-size black iced tea bags

1 cup (240 g) whiskey

1 large lemon, thinly sliced

—
Makes 6 to 8 servings

AT HOME: Bring the water to a boil in a large kettle. Remove the kettle from the heat and add the sugar and tea bags. Steep for about 5 minutes, stirring occasionally, until the sugar is dissolved.

Remove the tea bags, squeeze the liquid out, and discard. Let cool, then transfer the sweet tea to a half-gallon container. Stir in the whiskey and chill for up to 3 days.

IN CAMP: Serve the spiked sweet tea over ice and garnish with lemon slices.

Mimosa Sangria

Mimosa is why long, lazy mornings exist. Sangria is why long, lazy afternoons exist. Put them together and you might as well park yourself in that hammock for the rest of the day. What I like most about this recipe is that it's more of a loose guideline, open to endless variations, and hard to mess up. You can mix and match your favorite fruits, juices, and liqueurs to create a signature cocktail that's probably way too easy of a pour (or "highly drinkable," as they say in the booze world). Better make a double batch for brunch!

3 cups (700 ml) fruit juice

3 cups (750 g) fresh fruits (sliced or diced, if necessary)

½ cup (120 ml) fruity liqueur (such as Cointreau, Grand Marnier, or Chambord)

1 (750 ml) bottle dry sparkling wine, chilled

—
Makes 8 to 10 servings

Combine the juice, fruit, and liqueur in a large jar (or pitcher, if serving from one) and let the flavors intermingle for at least 1 hour. If you have space in your cooler, keep the mixture chilled until ready to use.

Add the sparkling wine to the jar (or pitcher) and serve immediately. Alternatively, you can fill individual glasses about one-third full with the juice mixture and top with sparkling wine.

3-2-1 Margarita

A classic margarita is an incredibly simple beverage to concoct: just tequila, triple sec, and lime juice. But when you want to keep it even simpler in the backcountry, limeade is a clever cheat that almost makes it taste like the real thing. Ratios for margaritas can vary but here's an easy one to remember in camp: 3 parts limeade, 2 parts tequila, and 1 part triple sec.

3 parts limeade

2 parts silver tequila

1 part triple sec

Jalapeño pepper, thinly sliced (optional)

—

Makes 1 serving

Combine the limeade, tequila, and triple sec in a glass and top off with ice. If you like your margarita with some heat, stir in a few slices of jalapeño before serving.

Paloma

Margaritas (right) may be the most well known of Mexico's cocktails on this side of the border, but the Paloma (left) tops the list as a traditional favorite in the country. Fizzy, invigorating, and smooth, it's exactly what you want on a hot, lazy, leisurely day by the water. You can try any brand of grapefruit soda, such as Izze, Hansen's, Blue Sky, San Pellegrino, or even Squirt or Fresca, but Jarritos is the most popular mixer, if you can find it.

1 part silver tequila

1 part grapefruit soda

Juice of ½ medium lime

Kosher salt

—

Makes 1 serving

Combine the tequila, grapefruit soda, and lime juice in a glass. Add a pinch of salt, top off with ice, and serve.

Ruby Red Grapefruit Shandy

English speakers know this drink as a shandy, but around the world it goes by a number of other monikers: panaché (France), clara (Spain), radler (Germany), and Sneeuwwitje ("Snow White" in Holland). Whatever you call it, there's no arguing that this refreshing beer cocktail is easy drinkin'. Though a few commercial breweries have packaged their own versions of shandies, it's a simple concoction to make in camp: just combine beer and juice. It's equally good for improving a beer you're not keen on, or enhancing a beer you already enjoy.

1 part light lager or wheat beer, chilled

1 part ruby red grapefruit juice, chilled

—

Makes 1 serving

Pour the beer into a glass, then top with the juice.

MIX IT UP

Try a variety of fruit juices and nectars to craft your own signature shandy, such as orange juice, pomegranate juice, mango nectar, pear nectar, apple cider, lemonade, or the Hawaiian blend of POG (passion fruit, orange, guava).

Summer Ale Sangria with Ginger and Peach

When you can't make up your mind between beer and sangria for happy hour, try a beer sangria—the happy-go-lucky, sun-kissed love child of two very respectable beverages. It's fresh, fruity, and fizzy, and makes the most of seasonal summer ales that show up for those few glorious months. Look for a light, bright, and crisp ale with notes of citrus or stone fruits to balance the spicy ginger beer and fresh ripe peaches.

Handful of fresh basil leaves

2 medium peaches, pitted and thinly sliced

2 (12-ounce/350 ml) bottles summer ale, chilled

1 cup (240 ml) ginger beer, chilled

1 cup (240 ml) peach nectar, chilled

—

Makes 4 servings

In a stockpot, muddle the basil and half the peaches. Add the remaining peaches and the ale, ginger beer, and peach nectar and stir to combine. Serve immediately. (Pictured right.)

MIX IT UP

If you're not traveling far, you can use sliced frozen peaches in place of fresh peaches to keep the sangria colder longer.

Honey Bourbon Lemonade

I like a good old-fashioned lemonade, but I love a good old-fashioned lemonade spiked with a shot of honey bourbon (such as Wild Turkey American Honey or Jim Beam Honey). The sweetness of the bourbon goes down smooth and adds just the right amount of booze to the kind of beverage you want to slowly swill all day by the lake. (Hey, nothing wrong with that.)

5 cups (12 dL) water, divided

1 cup (100 g) sugar

1 cup (240 ml) freshly squeezed lemon juice

1 cup (240 ml) honey bourbon

1 large lemon, thinly sliced

—

Makes 6 to 8 servings

AT HOME: Combine 2 cups (475 ml) of the water and the sugar in a small saucepan over medium heat. Stir until the sugar is dissolved, then remove from the heat and let the simple syrup cool to room temperature.

Pour the syrup, lemon juice, bourbon, and remaining 3 cups (725 ml) water into a half-gallon container. Depending on the acidity of your lemons, adjust for taste and add more sugar, lemon juice, or water as needed. Chill for up to 1 week.

IN CAMP: Serve the honey bourbon lemonade over ice and garnish with lemon slices.

Lemonade Love

A good lemonade starts with the above recipe of simple syrup, lemon juice, and water. Make it even better with one of the flavor variations below.

For Herbal Lemonade: Steep a few sprigs of thyme, rosemary, mint, or basil in the simple syrup over low heat for about 30 minutes. Discard the herbs and combine the infused syrup with lemon juice and water as directed above.

For Strawberry Lemonade: Add 1 cup strawberry puree to the lemonade. Or take it a step further and use a basil-infused syrup for Strawberry-Basil Lemonade.

For Pink Lemonade: Add 2 tablespoons grenadine to the lemonade.

For Spa Lemonade: Use a mint-infused syrup and steep sliced cucumbers in the lemonade for at least 2 hours (and no more than 2 days) before serving.

For Arnold Palmer: Replace the water with strong brewed green, black, or white tea.

For Limeade: Replace the lemon juice with freshly squeezed lime juice.

Camp Chai

It may not be the most authentic chai, but the ease of having a jar of homemade chai concentrate on hand for spicy mugs of tea in camp cannot be beat. The sweetened condensed milk slips some comfort into warm tea that's most welcome on a chilly morning when you don't even want to get out of your sleeping bag, much less your tent. Mix it with a robust, strong-brewed black tea, such as Assam, English breakfast, or Earl Grey, for a classic chai. If you want to mix it up, try a lighter tea like Darjeeling.

FOR THE CHAI CONCENTRATE

1 (14-ounce/415-ml) can sweetened condensed milk

1 teaspoon ground cardamom

1 teaspoon ground ginger

½ teaspoon ground cinnamon

½ teaspoon ground cloves

FOR THE CHAI

Black tea bag

Hot water

—

Makes up to 14 servings

AT HOME: To make the chai concentrate, combine all of the ingredients in a small bowl. Transfer to a lidded container and chill for up to 3 weeks.

IN CAMP: Steep the tea bag in a mug of hot water for 3 to 5 minutes. Stir in a few spoonfuls of chai concentrate to taste.

MIX IT UP

Cardamom, ginger, cinnamon, and cloves are the core ingredients of any good chai, but you can customize the spice mix to your liking—try star anise, fennel, allspice, coriander, or even black pepper if you're feeling adventurous.

Homemade Hot Chocolate Mix

Those little packets of hot cocoa mix—you know, the ones with the dehydrated mini marshmallows in them—have a certain nostalgia that I sometimes can't resist.

1 cup (170 g) bittersweet chocolate chips, very finely chopped (at least 60% cacao)

1 cup (85 g) unsweetened cocoa powder

1 cup (100 g) sugar

½ cup (21 g) dry milk powder

½ teaspoon kosher salt

—
Makes 14 to 18 servings

Combine all of the ingredients in a small bowl. Transfer to an airtight container and store in a dry, cool place for up to 3 months.

CLASSIC HOT CHOCOLATE

1 cup (240 ml) water or milk

3 to 4 tablespoons Homemade Hot Chocolate Mix (left)

—
Makes 1 serving

Heat the water in a small saucepan over medium heat until steamy. Add the hot chocolate mix and stir until all of the ingredients are dissolved and well blended.

MEXICAN HOT CHOCOLATE

1 cup (240 ml) water or milk

3 to 4 tablespoons Homemade Hot Chocolate Mix (above)

⅛ teaspoon ground cinnamon

Pinch of ground cayenne pepper

—
Makes 1 serving

Heat the water in a small saucepan over medium heat until steamy. Add the hot chocolate mix, cinnamon, and cayenne and stir until all of the ingredients are dissolved and well blended.

SNUGGLERS

1 part peppermint schnapps

6 parts Classic Hot Chocolate (opposite page)

—
Makes 1 serving

Stir the schnapps into a mug of hot chocolate until well combined.

Citrus and Maple Mulled Wine

Mulled wine is one of those things where everyone has a certain way of making it, and usually with a secret ingredient, kind of like barbecue sauce or the family pot roast. So, here's my secret ingredient: maple syrup. In the past, I'd always used sugar to sweeten the brew (because steeping brings out the sour tannic flavor in wine), but I found that maple syrup adds a deep, smooth sweetness that takes the mulled wine to another level. It pairs especially well with wines that have hints of dark fruit, like plum, currant, and blackberry. Go with a syrup on the darker side of the spectrum, such as Grade A: Dark Color Robust Flavor for its strong, almost brown sugar–like flavor.

2 (750 ml) bottles red wine

½ cup (120 ml) maple syrup

1 teaspoon coriander seeds

2 (3-inch/8-cm) cinnamon sticks

12 allspice berries

2 star anise

1 bay leaf

2 medium oranges, halved crosswise

½ cup (120 ml) brandy

—
Makes 8 servings

Add the wine, maple syrup, and all of the spices to a stockpot over medium heat. Juice the oranges into the stockpot and add the rinds. Bring to a simmer, reduce the heat to low, and steep for at least 30 minutes to let the flavors develop. Stir in the brandy before serving and ladle into mugs, avoiding the orange rinds and spices.

WAKE UP THOSE SPICES

To bring out even deeper flavor in your spices, toast them in the stockpot over medium-high heat before adding the other ingredients.

Vanilla and Bourbon Mulled Cider

Warm and fragrant, this mulled cider sings with heady spices (and a hint of booze) without overwhelming the delicate apple aroma. It's more than just swirling in a few cinnamon sticks or tossing in a bag of generic "mulling spices." Having the right blend of spice helps balance and enhance the natural acidity and sweetness in the apples, and if you start with great cider, you'll end up with great mulled cider. Look for one that's deep in color and cloudy with good body.

1 quart (1 L) apple cider

2 (3-inch/8-cm) cinnamon sticks

4 cardamom pods, bruised with the side of a knife

4 cloves

¼ teaspoon coriander seeds

½ vanilla bean, split

½ cup (120 ml) bourbon

—
Makes 4 servings

Add the cider and all of the spices to a small saucepan over medium heat. Bring to a simmer, reduce the heat to low, and steep for at least 30 minutes to let the flavors develop. Stir in the bourbon before serving and ladle into mugs, avoiding the spices.

About the Author

After many miles traveled in pursuit of adventure, countless meals shared under the open sky, and a decade of growing her own food and raising backyard chickens, Linda Ly truly believes a life outdoors is a life well lived. Whether she's grilling, gardening, snowboarding, mountain biking, or exploring her new stomping grounds of the Pacific Northwest, there are few days where the snow or the rain keeps her inside. Linda writes about all these simple pleasures, as well as her evolving modern homestead, on her award-winning blog *Garden Betty*.

In the fall of 2017, Linda and her husband, Will Taylor, and their daughter, Gemma Lumen, moved to their dream town of beautiful Bend, Oregon. It was the best decision they ever made for their family.

Follow along on www.gardenbetty.com and www.thebackyardfirecookbook.com. And don't forget to check out the companion book, *The New Camp Cookbook*, if you agree everything just tastes better outside.

About the Photographer

While a love of photography budded at an early age, Will Taylor's true passion and image-making career all started one evening capturing the sun's setting rays across the stunning expanse of Lake Tahoe, high in the Sierra Nevada Mountains. With the click of the shutter, Will realized the inherent power of photography to freeze a moment in time and then project that place, that instance, to others, sharing the beauty and inspiration of that split second. That one photo launched Will into his new career, and now,

decades later, he still captures the beauty of our natural world for clients ranging from Fortune 500 companies to the world's top fashion brands.

For Will's latest outdoor adventures in his new home in Central Oregon, where you'll find him mountain biking and snowboarding through the majestic beauty of the Cascade Mountains with his wife and daughter, visit www.instagram.com/willtaylorphotography.

Index

CPSIA information can be obtained
at www.ICGtesting.com
Printed in the USA
JSHW041732300423
40830JS00006B/7